THE COMPLETE MAILING LIST TOOLKIT

BARB DROZDOWICH

2nd edition

ebook ISBN: 978-1-988821-35-1

Print ISBN: 978-1-988821-36-8

I would like to thank you for buying one of my books!

I tend to focus on the technical tasks that authors and bloggers need to learn. As of this publishing I have 27 books in print and several more in various stages of completion. I'm always looking to be helpful - often creating books around subjects that I get a lot of questions on from authors and bloggers just like you.

At the end of this book is the link join my group of readers and get some free help with the technical subjects.

On to the book - I hope you enjoy and learn lots!

CONTENTS

BOOK 3 - NEWSLETTERS THAT ROCK

INTRODUCTION

Welcome to "*The Complete Mailing List Toolkit*," part of an ongoing series of author 'how-to' books, which is designed to help you navigate the technical issues of self-publishing. This "toolkit" specifically focuses on how to create optimized reader newsletters, how to grow your mailing list, and how to ensure your newsletter arrives in inboxes.

I will use the word 'Communication' a lot in this book. I feel to be successfully engaged with your audience, you must communicate with them, not simply bombard them with email and social media posts. Whereas many experts focus on simply gaining subscribers, I argue that this is too narrow of a focus.

Why this book?

Two reasons:

1) This book is well researched and pulls information from many different schools of thought and

2) I take a holistic view of communicating with readers.

Initially, my intention with this collection of books was to collect information from a wide variety of sources and condense it into a neat and easy to understand package for you. However, as I was researching, my opinion changed. I found that much of the information available online and in various webinars seemed to miss the boat in terms of accuracy, while others just seemed fixated on adding people to a mailing list like hoarders would add one more item to a collection. They weren't looking at their readers as individuals, nor were they treating them as such. I wanted to create something more "big picture-ish" (is that a word?) – that looks at all aspects and all facets, of communicating with readers using newsletters. Hence this book. For authors who just want to attack one part of this puzzle, the books are available individually, but my wish is that they are all read together.

I come from a background of technical training and while I'm certainly comfortable with technology, I tend to be holistic in my view. I want to break subjects down into manageable sections, and I don't want to skip topics because they are difficult to explain. I feel that I haven't done my job unless I can explain complicated things and make them relevant to you. I'm holistic in terms of looking at one subject within a larger context.

In terms of communicating with readers, I don't focus on only one part of the puzzle in this group of books. I want you to understand why I suggest using shorter subject lines for a newsletter. I want you to understand why entertaining readers, is as important as communicating with them. I want you to understand why it is necessary to use an Email Marketing System right from the get go to communicate with readers. I want you to understand how to work within the laws that govern your actions when you communicate with readers. I want to explain why the technical aspects that many overlook are really important to success in your endeavors.

Most importantly, I want you to understand that there isn't a one size fits all method of communication. The way you communicate with a teenager isn't the way you would communicate with a senior. The material that fans of romance are interested in is not likely to be the same as fans of horror. I want you to learn what your audience wants, not take the advice of an expert without thinking about it and without testing it out. I want you to learn to talk WITH your audience, not AT your audience. I want you to see your readers as more than a wallet.

Seems like I have a huge objective! We are going to break the subject of communicating with readers down into four books. In the first book we are going to address the topic of gathering the names of interested readers. We're going to view it as something other than hoarding.

In the second book we're going to talk about making sure that our newsletters actually end up in the inbox of our readers. This book will be fairly technical, but you'll have a good understanding of why best practices are what they are.

Finally, in the last book, we're going to talk about how to create really great content that is appropriate for our readers. We'll bring in some science, some psychology, and some good old-fashioned marketing to help you form a plan for going forward.

I guess it is too soon to say that I've really enjoyed writing these books...but I hope that you appreciate my efforts and learn to be better communicators with your readers!

Onward...

BARB DROZDOWICH

INTRODUCTION

In this first book we are going to talk about growing your mailing list, but since I feel the real power is in communicating effectively with whomever joins your list, more emphasis will be put on the communication sections of this book. However, we will start at the beginning – growing your list.

First of all, why focus on a mailing list and newsletter?

Many studies suggest that newsletters or communication via email is the most successful method of communication. It is even more popular than social media. In a study by IPSOS, nearly 85% of people who use the Internet, use email, compared to only 62% who use social networking sites. If we look at these numbers in a slightly different way, studies will show that engagement rates for Twitter and Facebook are generally in the range of 1 to 2%. The engagement rate on newsletters or email can be as high as 50 to 60% depending on the study performed.

Regardless of how you want to look at the numbers, email or newsletters are seen as more personal and more targeted than anything that appears on social media. People are very conservative about handing out an email address. Getting access to someone's email is almost like getting the keys to the kingdom. People tend to only give out that information if they feel they will be interested in what you have to share.

In my experience, growing a mailing list can be one of the most frustrating parts about actually communicating with your readers. Often, an endless amount of time is spent trying to figure out how to convince people to hand over their email addresses. In part one of this book, we're going to learn strategies to grow your list that have been drawn from all parts of the marketplace but we're also going to talk about some common sense information and ensure you haven't over-looked any core marketing principles.

One point to make before we move on – as I suggested in the introduction to this book, I feel the fixation with adding names to a list is like hoarding. Names or email addresses are useless unless you communicate and they respond. We'll be focusing on all the parts of this puzzle, one at a time. For now, I'll leave you with an interesting quote from Kirsten Oliphant in a post on Jane Friedman's blog (http://janefriedman.com/grow-email-list/):

> " The 10,000 subscriber mark seems to be the magic number. This is where agents and publishers take notice of non-fiction authors. Nick Stevenson heralds this number in his 'Your first 10,000 K' course."

Kirsten goes on to comment that numbers aren't the answer to everything. 10,000 subscribers are nothing if they don't want to engage. I agree with her!

1

HOW TO ENCOURAGE PEOPLE TO JOIN YOUR LIST.

Let's start with how to encourage people to join your list. What do people need to make that decision?

This can be broken down into three parts:

1) People have to be clear about what they will be getting.
2) People are attracted to quality content.
3) It has to be easy to join your mailing list.

Part 1) People have to be clear about what they will be getting

People have to be clear about what they will be getting in order for them to be willing to enter their email address/name. As I'm sure you are aware, there are many different things that we can subscribe to: online magazine subscriptions, blog posts, mailing lists, membership sites, just to name a few.

Since the main topic of this book is mailing lists and newsletters we're going to ignore every type of subscription except mailing lists. However, knowing there are many different kinds of subscriptions, if your signup form simply says 'Subscribe Now' or 'Join My List,' are you really being clear about what the person is subscribing to or joining?

Take a few moments to go to your site and look at what the words say on the widget or form you use to get subscribers. Have a look and see if what they actually get is what is described or stated. In other words if a person enters an email address do they just get your newsletters, or do you think they would appreciate getting your blog posts also? If so, do you tell them that that is what they are going to get?

Do you want to offer your subscribers choices? So, for example, do you want to have a series of checkboxes on your sign-up form that will allow people to state their preferences? You can have a form that collects an email address, first name and then asks subscribers to check the box beside the type of news they want to get.

Another way of doing the same thing is polling your subscribers after they have joined and asking them what they want. Two different points of view, and I'm sure, that everybody will have an opinion on the difference between the two.

The common train of thought is to ask people for as little information as possible to prevent them from having second thoughts and backing away before subscribing. Because of this, often subscribers are only asked for their email address. We will come back to the subject of what to ask for during the subscription process in a later book. If you share this concern, you may not be willing to include checkboxes in your subscription form or widget. The problem with polling your subscribers after they have already joined your list is getting everyone to respond. As we will talk about in a future book, all newsletters have deliverability issues, and all humans have the ability to choose whether or not to open an email.

. . .

This gives you a point to think about – your first bit of homework if you will. Decide what you want to do going forward with your subscription form design. I actually don't feel that there is a right answer. I think that you need to do what is best for your audience. Potentially trial and error will guide you to the best choice based on your unique audience.

> A point that will come up frequently in this book is: "People who are unhappy with what they are getting will react in a way that you won't like." In a future book we will talk about people declaring your newsletter to be spam when in actual fact all they want to do is unsubscribe. Ultimately people who are not clear about what they will be getting will not be happy on your list. Unhappy people are not willing to be participatory and the name of the game with newsletters is participation from readers.

Part 2) People are attracted to quality content

Recently an author asked me how he was supposed to **make** people sign up to his mailing list. He was a new author with a new blog. If memory serves he had three posts. His sign-up form said "Subscribe Now" and the button said "Join Now." My response to him was twofold. First, you aren't telling people what they are joining or subscribing to. Second, you only have three posts. If people make the assumption that they are subscribing to your blog posts, there is no history of quality content (or not much). If they take a leap and assume that they are joining a mailing list, there is no indication of what they are in for. Needless to say, this author was offended by my comments.

Put yourself in the shoes of your readers. They theoretically don't know you from Adam. They certainly don't want their inbox flooded with crap. If you were looking at a blog with three posts and being asked to subscribe with no indication of what you were subscribing to, would you?

. . .

I know I wouldn't.

This takes us back to the idea of letting people know what they will be getting if they subscribe. Even if you aren't overly clear with your subscription form or widget, they may look at your body of work; in fact, they may be on your blog because you answered a question for them in one of your posts, and decide to take a chance on you. Readers may decide that you have a body of work, a collection of quality posts on subjects that they're interested in reading about, and are interested in giving your subscription a try.

The quality content that is judged may not just be on your blog. There are three basic sources of "quality content." The first source, which we talked about above, is a blog with a history of quality posts. The second source is a signup form or link in the front and or back matter of a book you have written. Someone may read your book and decide it is enough indication of quality content to encourage a sign-up to your mailing list. The third source is to offer a free item. This free item may encourage a potential subscriber to take a chance on your mailing list without any indication of what they will get or in fact, the quality of the free item. Most readers are aware that it should be quite easy to unsubscribe if their expectations are not met by whatever the free item is.

Let's talk about sign-ups in the front matter or back matter of a book. If you have written a book, make sure that there are clear points of sign-up to your newsletter certainly in the back matter of your book and potentially in the front matter as well. This is something that is easier to do in e-books than it is in paperbacks, as an e-book can have a hyperlink directly to the sign up form. Even paperbacks can have mention of signing up for a mailing list on your website, however.

There's a marketing term known as "warm lead." Someone who

has just finished reading your book hopefully is really impressed by your content. If you catch them before they get busy and wander away you can get a “warm lead” or an interested person neatly signed up to your mailing list. As we'll talk about in other sections of this chapter, make sure that it is easy to join your mailing list. Don't make the instructions too complicated; don't send the potential new sign up on a goose chase to find the link to sign up. We all know that clickable links can be put in e-books. But not everybody reads an e-book on a device that will allow them to move away from the e-book to a browser in order to access a signup form. Devices such as a basic Kindle e-reader will have limitations. Because of this, make sure that if you are going to include a clickable link, that you also include a simple link that they can manually type into their computer’s browser window, or simply send them to your website to look for the bright yellow form, or some other similar landmark.

The third point that I brought up is to offer something for free. Many people that I know are unwilling to give away a book for free, or they are traditionally published and their publisher refuses to grant them the right to give away a book. This seems to be a sticking point with many folk. So, in my opinion, do you need to give away something to entice people to join your mailing list? If you are just starting out and have little to no track record, you absolutely do. Again, put yourself in the shoes of your potential subscribers. How likely are you to give away your email address for the sake of getting something free?

Does the item that you're giving away have to be a whole book? No, of course not. Generally speaking, experts suggest that the free item be something of value that would be attractive to your audience and, if at all possible, be something your audience can't easily get elsewhere. Put your creative hat on and come up with something unique. I've heard of a thriller writer offering a realistic looking dossier on the bad guy of their book. I've heard of romance writers offering an excerpt to their up and coming new release. Neither of these options would cause objection even if you are a traditionally published author.

Both of these choices would be attractive to the audience - something that they can't get anywhere else yet will be something that they are willing to give up their email address to get.

Here's your next bit of homework: What can you offer your readers as an enticement to join your mailing list? If you only have one book written or are having to follow rules from your publisher, what can you create relatively easily to offer as enticement?

Part 3) It has to be easy to join.

Regardless of where people join your list, it needs to be easy, it needs to be obvious, and it needs to be consistent across your platform. There is that phrase that people don't like to talk about - an author's platform. When I say an author's platform, what I'm meaning is all of the various places that you have a presence both on-line and off-line. Most people can figure out that they need to put a sign-up form or widget on their website, perhaps in the front and back matter of their book, but they forget about all of the other places that they have a presence.

I'm going to break this section down into six categories:

1) Website

As I was doing the research for this book I found an article that claimed that sign-up forms get ignored when they are in the sidebar area of a blog or website. They called this phenomenon "sidebar blindness." A cool term and something I hadn't really thought about before. In reality if I'm searching for information or reading blog posts, I am absolutely capable of ignoring a blog's sidebar. So, if we can agree that sidebar blindness exists, let's talk about some of the other places on a website or a blog that a sign-up form or widget can be put.

As we work through this list, consider the fact that mailing list sign-ups don't only have to be in one location. They can be put in a variety of places.

a) Have a sign-up form embedded in a bar that hovers at the top or bottom of your site. These bars tend to be a brighter color to stand out from the rest of the content of the blog.

b) Have a banner that exists just below the header of your site. This location is quite obvious and typically is a strip of color to stand out from the rest of the body of the blog.

c) Have the sign-up form embedded within the body of a blog post. This can exist in a number of different ways. There can perhaps be an embedded form at the bottom of each post, as part of the sign off or signature of the post. Or part of the sign off or signature of the blog post can have an embedded text link that connects to a sign-up form in a different location.

d) Have a sign-up link as part of the author information box. Most blogs will allow for a customized author biography and social media links to appear at the bottom of every blog post. It's possible to either have a sign-up icon or simply a text link to a sign-up form existing elsewhere.

e) Have a pop-up sign-up form that appears after the reader has been on the blog for a period of time. Pop-up sign-up forms are a bit iffy these days because of two factors. First of all, from a technical stand-point, Google has specific rules that came into effect in 2017. A link to Google's rules about pop-ups can be found here

(https://webmasters.googleblog.com/2016/08/helping-users-easily-access-content-on.html)

and I've written about it on my blog.

(http://bakerviewconsulting.com/2016/10/demystifying-googles-new-popup-rules/)

According to Google's new rules a pop-up can't appear immediately, and it can't block the majority of the screen. It can however slide up from the bottom or slide in from the side covering a small fraction of the screen. Secondly, there are strong feelings about pop-ups in the blogging world. Some people hate them, some feel that they are the key to getting people to sign up to a mailing list. What is your opinion? I'm always up for trying new things – carefully. If you are interested in popups, give them a try but watch the stats on your site and see if people are just leaving instead of filling in their email address.

f) Have a landing page. Technically, a landing page and a home page are essentially the same thing. Many people have a static landing page which is the first thing that visitors see when they come to a website. This can be something that is viewed yet can be scrolled beyond to see the rest of the content of the site, or a landing page can be all there is to see. Again, different perspectives. If you have books to give away, a nice display of free books with text encouraging visitors to enter an email address so that you know where to deliver the free books can be very attractive to some. It can also be a bit off-putting to some people. What I like is in the middle of the road. I like to create informative landing pages that have an obvious mailing list sign-up point, yet have other information about the author and their books as well. Look around at various examples of websites in your genre. See what you like and what you don't like. It is possible to create a commercial landing page using something like Leadpages.net. But most blog themes these days will allow for a very attractive motivating landing page to be created without needing much help.

. . .

How ever you present a sign-up point on your website/blog make sure it is attractive, clear and consider posting a few testimonials from happy mailing list people or some other form of social proof to encourage other sign-ups. Also consider posting previous newsletters on your website so that interested people can see what they will be getting if they enter their email address.

2)Books and/or Courses

As we've mentioned before, all of your books should have at least one sign up point to your mailing list. Typically it can be found in the back matter of the book. I've also seen examples of a teaser being put in the front matter of a book as well. We have also mentioned giving away a free book in order to get someone to sign up for your mailing list.

Let's talk about this free item further. How can people find out about the item that you're giving away for free? As we mentioned in the previous section it can be part of the sign up verbiage on your website. It can also be offered as what's called the lead magnet in your book(s) as part of the sign-up incentive to the mailing list.

There are commercial sites that will facilitate you giving away a free book in exchange for a sign up on your mailing list. My favorite right now is Bookfunnel.com. This site will allow you to upload a copy of what you're giving away for free and collect email addresses from those who take a few copy. This giveaway link can be advertised in many different places. You can share it on social media, you can include it at the bottom of blog posts - wherever you can think to share this link that people will find out about it.

If you offer a course or a free workshop or webinar, there are many different companies that will allow you to either host recorded videos, or host a live video, and collect names and email addresses of every one who takes the course. You need to be careful of the permission issue in this situation. Many of the free webinars I've attended make it clear that signing up for the training will involve signing up for a mailing list.

. . .

An interesting idea, that I saw a few weeks ago, was the offer to give somebody a free book, (electronic, not paperback copy) in exchange for proof of a purchase of another one. A "Pay It Forward" type of idea. There are many different ways to do this, but if you offered to give away a free copy of book number two with proof of purchase of book number one, you have an email address. If you offer to give away a free book to a friend of someone who has proof of purchase of one of your books you have an email address. Although this idea is interesting I would be careful using these email addresses, as the person really hasn't given permission. They might be a fan but they might also be annoyed to hear from you.

However, if you have a link to your mailing list along with the little blurb as part of your email signature, any email communication with potential readers can allow them to make the choice to sign up for your mailing list.

3) Social Media

The various social media platforms will allow for sign-up forms or widgets to be put in place. Probably the most obvious is Facebook. Facebook actually has a call to action button that can be directed at your mailing list.

Every one of the major social media platforms will allow you to create a bio. Some of the bios are short, some are longer. Regardless of the length, it is possible to put a 'Call to Action' in all of the bios instructing people to join your mailing list.

On both your Facebook page and Twitter stream, you can pin a tweet or a post with a Call to Action encouraging people to join your mailing list. Most Facebook groups have rules about self-promotion, but many will allow self-promotion on certain days or in certain ways. In groups where this is allowed, encourage sign-ups to your mailing list. Perhaps create a cool little graphic on Canva or some other graphic program along with a text statement that encourages signing-up for your mailing list.

You can pin your Opt-in page on Pinterest.

If you have created a YouTube video, let's say a book trailer, make sure that the creator of the trailer puts a Call to Action to your mailing list at the end of the video.

If you find LinkedIn to be an active part of your on-line presence, add information about your mailing list to your bio there. If you are known to be knowledgeable in various groups - answering questions and the like - people may be attracted to your mailing list.

A very common activity on social media is a Rafflecopter give-away. A Rafflecopter is a great way to host a giveaway, collect email addresses as well as new social media contacts. If you are going to gather email addresses this way though, make sure you are clear about what you are going to use the addresses for. I've been witness to too many groups that feel they can hand out lists of email address without properly informing entrants. This tends to result in high complaint numbers. And in today's rule filled world, this sort of behavior can get you in trouble.

4) Online events or in-person events

There are a lot of online promotional activities that many authors take part in. From Facebook parties, to Twitter chats, to chat rooms of various descriptions. All of these will allow you the opportunity to share various pieces of information. Generally speaking, in these situations, we don't hesitate to share the URL of our website or other social media platform URLs. I encourage you to include links to your mailing list. If you are doing an in person event such as a book signing or a meet and greet with an author group, be ready with business cards, or my favorite, my iPad with the sign-up form that connects directly with MailChimp. Honestly even a piece of paper and a pen works just fine to collect information.

. . .

5) Other Online Platforms

What I'm referring to in this section is the various places that you appear online that aren't yours. When you are a guest on a podcast make sure the host is aware of all of the various places that you can be found online including your mailing list. If you share a guest post on another blog, make sure that you include your contact information at the bottom of the post. Again, include your mailing list, not just the obvious contact points. There are other places where we can share information online. From Huff Post to Medium, to WattPad, if you are going to share information, make sure you include information about your contact points and your mailing list. Many commentators in the industry talk about what is frequently called "Byline Blindness" - the result of an over saturation of guest bloggers. If in fact you are going to guest blog make sure that your contact information is within the text of your guest post – not just as an "Author Box" appearing at the end of your post.

6) Things that don't fit anywhere else

If you think about it, there are a lot of opportunities to find people to add to your mailing list. Anybody that you talk to in person can be encouraged to join your mailing list. Do I suggest automatically adding all of your Gmail contacts to your mailing list? No. That fits in the category of pissing people off! But don't hesitate to encourage people already on your mailing list to refer their friends perhaps to win a prize. There are a variety of opportunities to run ads, both online and off-line. There certainly is the popular Facebook ads to encourage sign-ups, but have you considered including something in your local writers group newsletter, or a genre specific literary magazine? Put your creative hat on and I'm sure that you'll find all kinds of places to mention your mailing list.

CONCLUSION

Let's talk about some final comments about growing your mailing list. HubSpot, which is a leading marketing website, suggests that your email list degrades by about 22½% per year. People change jobs and therefore email addresses and in fact, people change private email providers. So you can assume that just over a fifth of the people that you sign up to your newsletter won't be reachable in a year.

There are two ways of looking at this. Many people try to find strategies to reengage their list. We'll talk about some of these in the last book of this collection, but you might want to consider having a section of your newsletter that reminds people if they are planning on changing their email address to let you know and you can add a new email address to your list manually. In fact, most Email Marketing Services will automatically put an 'Update Preferences' link in the footer of your note – typically right near the 'Unsubscribe' link. This will allow your subscribers to change their own email address on your list. Most importantly, if you have great content, people will miss your newsletter when they forget to tell you that they're changing email addresses and will come and find you.

BOOK 2 - GET YOUR EMAILS DELIVERED

GET YOUR EMAILS DELIVERED

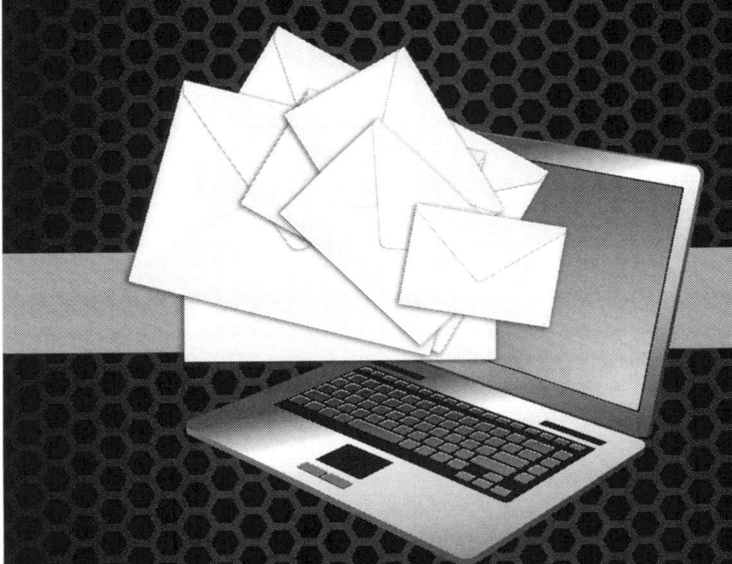

BARB DROZDOWICH

INTRODUCTION

Why should you care about Deliverability? And what is that anyway?

Deliverability is getting emails into inboxes.

You are likely saying to yourself - Duh…an email is sent and it's received. Ta-dah - easy peasy!

Actually, not so easy as we'll find out. In this book we are going to talk about getting emails into the inboxes of our readers - not the spam folders. We're going to learn about bounces, open rates and click through rates and why you should care about these things.

Just to throw out some numbers - did you know that about a fifth of all opt-in emails that are sent don't arrive into inboxes? That's a general number covering all sorts of industries and not necessarily specific to authors, but it gives you an idea that sending newsletters isn't as simple as clicking on the send button. Of that 20% mentioned above some will end up in spam folders but some will bounce and not arrive at their destination at all.

By the end of this book, you'll learn how and why an email doesn't get to where it should go and you'll also learn how to combat some of the common problems. We'll also cover some preventative measures to help keep your mailing list fresh.

We're going to start with some definitions - I'll see if I can take some complicated topics and break them down into easy to follow chunks. We're then going to end this book with some actionable items that will make a difference for your newsletter right away.

1

DEFINE DELIVERABILITY

I think people generally assume that email is just automatically delivered to the address that we send it to. My research tells me this is not true. As I stated in the Introduction, about 20% of all opt-in emails never make it to the inbox. You'll notice that I specify opt-in emails. In this book we are specifically talking about emails that are newsletters, so that is what we're mostly interested in. But as an aside, studies show that newsletter delivery generally is not 100%.

When we're talking about deliverability we need to be clear what is meant by that word. A quote from *Email Delivery Best Practices Guide* – a part of the MailChimp help documentation.

> "Successful email delivery is your message arriving in the inbox of the recipient as intended. Email delivery failure is when your message is either validated to the junk or spam folder, or completely blocked by an Internet service provider."

What are bounced emails? A bounced email is one that isn't successfully sent for a variety of reasons. Bounces can be classified as either soft or hard bounces. A hard bounce happens when an email is sent to an email address that doesn't exist for some reason. Either it did and has since been closed or there is an error in the email address resulting in no known address. There's no easy recovery from a hard bounce other than contacting the person and requesting a new email address.

A soft bounce, on the other hand, can be easier to recover from. A soft bounce can just be a notification that there is a bit of difficulty in delivery but it will resolve itself.

There are a variety of reasons for a newsletter to bounce - hard or soft. Here are the most common ones:

1) A non-existent email address - if an email account has been closed or deleted the email will get a hard bounce. This type of bounce occurs when subscribers close old email accounts or move jobs causing their work email address to be deleted. It is also possible that people give a false email address or make a mistake when submitting at a live event - perhaps filling out a paper form (although double opt-in will eliminate those errors)

2) Undeliverable email - notes in this category indicate that either the recipient's server is temporarily unavailable or was overloaded or under maintenance. This type of bounce may be recoverable from if the issue is temporary - as in maintenance - but if the email server is gone for good, the email will then hard bounce.

3) Mailbox is full - this is a common error for limited free email accounts. There is a cap on storage and the person has exceeded it. This can mean that the person has abandoned the address or they have maybe gone on holidays and will empty the mailbox when they get back.

4) Vacation/out of office reply - Unlike other bounce categories, these emails are usually delivered. Of course, someone who never returns from a vacation, will eventually be considered to be a hard bounce.

. . .

5) **Blocked email** - if your email address, or your email marketing service's email address has been blocked by the recipient's email program, the block needs to be requested to be removed. It isn't unusual for government or schools to have really tight reigns when it comes to receiving emails resulting in this type of a bounce.

6) **Denied by the Firewall or Spam Filter** - as we'll learn in this book, the recipient's email provider may decide that your note doesn't pass muster and is denied entry. This will result in a bounce as well. Sometimes the recipient adding your email address to their contact list will help, but there could be something in one newsletter's content that the firewall or spam filter finds objectionable and that situation can change for the next newsletter.

Bounce rates should be monitored - sudden increases should be paid attention to rather than accepted as normal. There will always be a certain number of bounces from a large list, but sudden changes are not normal.

2

DEFINE SPAM

The word spam is used in many different ways by many different people. Let's talk about some of these definitions. Typically the word spam refers to an unwanted email, an email that arrives in the inbox that wasn't requested. It can also refer to an email that contains content that is unwanted or offensive. I'm sure you know that type of email that I'm talking about. It contains advertisements for male enhancement products, casual hookups, and the like.

As I'm sure you are aware, there is the legal definition of spam as well as the common definitions of spam. And clearly, we overuse the word spam. As I stated above, the word spam can be used to refer to unwanted email as well as no longer wanted email but also it can refer to email that is clearly sent out in large numbers - the blanket type of mass marketed email. So by that definition newsletters can be spam. The same email is sent out to large numbers of people - that's by definition spam.

However, what makes newsletters more acceptable is that the recipients have opted into the newsletter as opposed to receiving the email against their will. But this helps us understand the actions of recipients of emails or newsletters. Most email programs have a button that can be clicked to indicate that the email is junk or spam. This really doesn't do anything definitive to stop the email from arriving, but many people don't actually know that. What it does is send a message through the email firewall to your email marketing service registering a complaint. This complaint can harm the deliverability of your emails or newsletters, and if enough of them are received, you can get sanctioned by your email marketing service.

One of the things that we will talk about shortly is the fact that it is a good idea to train or educate your readers. Let them know up front how to stop getting your newsletters if they no longer want them. Make it easy for them to do it gracefully. Don't leave them without an option other than to click the junk or spam button.

3

WHAT IS USER ENGAGEMENT?

User engagement - This is a term that is often just thrown about. When it comes to email, however it refers to if, and how, your readers engage with your newsletter. The thing is, the big email systems monitor how much the people who receive your newsletters interact with them. Do they open them, do they spend time reading them, do they scroll down to the bottom, do they ever reply or do they file them away in a folder for safekeeping? Do they add you to their contact list if they have Gmail? Do they drag your emails into their primary inbox tab? Or do your emails just sit unopened and unloved?

Every different email provider has its own way of judging whether emails are being engaged with. And no one outside of those providers actually know what's being looked for. But generally speaking, if overall your emails aren't being opened and read then it's going to be harder and harder for you to get your newsletter into the primary inbox in the future. Generalities can be made, however, how do you increase engagement? You can start by asking people to add your email address to their contact list.

In email delivery terms low open rates are a clear signal to the powers that be that your recipients are not engaged with you or your brand or your content. That lack of engagement is a factor in the delivery of future emails and can even lead to your campaigns being blocked. Think of it as a snowball threatening to become an avalanche.

Many people suggest deleting contacts if they don't seem to be engaging. There are also experts that don't believe in doing this. Consider the buying cycle of books. Isn't there a saying that a book/product has to be seen or mentioned seven times before a person will buy? Perhaps that time hasn't come. Perhaps your readers need more encouragement.

We will talk about methods to increase engagement, but on the surface, periodically send out a reminder to your readers to add your email address to their contact list or if they have Gmail to drag the newsletter out of the promotions column.

4

EMAIL LEGALITIES

As I've mentioned several times in this book, most countries have a form anti-spam legislation – laws that as senders of newsletters we need to follow. What we are going to do in this chapter is talk about the laws in generalities and use specific examples of how to avoid breaking any of these laws without getting into the weeds of the details of each country's version.

If I go back a few years, most authors would be roughly familiar with the CAN-SPAM act – which is the name of the legislation from the US. With the more recent GDPR legislation out of the UK, this topic has become more familiar to most authors.

Let's start this discussion with some broad stripes. The laws that we need to follow when we send out newsletters can fit into two categories: Opt-in laws and Opt-out laws. I'll define.

An Opt-in law requires permission from the receiver of an email or newsletter before their name is added to a mailing list or before you are allowed to communicate with them. An Opt-out law allows for names to be added without permission, but if requested, a name must be removed asap from a list and communication with that person needs to stop.

As of the writing of this book, the US law is considered to be an Opt-out law and the rest of the world's versions are considered to be Opt-in laws.

Let's add another piece of information to this discussion – you are prosecuted (or fined) by the country of the complainant – of the person who complains. Because of this, you need to follow ALL the laws, not just the ones that apply to the country you live in. Are authors frequently fined? No not really, but it does happen in my experience. What will happen more commonly is the various newsletter services like Mailerlite will respond to a body of complaints and sanction an account.

One more piece of information before we move on to some details – a common misconception is that the anti-spam laws only refer to promotional emails that are sent from big companies – like Best Buy or Nike. This isn't true. Generally speaking, these laws refer to any electronic communications. Practically, will you get in trouble for sending a personal email to a friend of a friend without advanced permission? Likely not. However, permission to communicate and permission to retain personal information is at the heart of most of the legislation so be mindful of that as you communicate with people.

Let's move on to the 4 points we are going to highlight in this chapter:

1) Obtain permission to communicate

2) Don't use deceptive headers or header graphics for your newsletter. Don't use deceptive subject lines or deceptive reply-to addresses

3) Always provide an unsubscribe link or an easy method of unsubscribing

4) Always include your physical mailing address

Obtain Permission to Communicate 

Permission is at the heart of most of the various legislations we need to follow. When we make use of newsletter services like Mailer-lite, this is worked into their functionality. Most of the newsletter services have the ability to use "double opt-in" during the sign-up process. This involves the newsletter service sending an email to the person's email address that requires an action to finalize the signup process. There is a button to click on or a link to click on that allows the person to confirm that they want their information to be added to your list. Without this final step, any email address can be added and potentially people can be added without permission.

As we talk about several times in this book, we want an audience that is participatory – who wants to be there. This whole name of the game with newsletters is to ultimately get people to interact with your newsletters and hopefully buy some of your books.

Don't use deceptive headers or header graphics. 

The header is the top area of a newsletter and it is either graphical or text based. What this point in the legislations is saying is don't pretend to be someone else. Most authors don't attempt this. They want their readers to figure out who they are. They use a graphic that is branded and helps the audience make the connection between them and their books quickly.

Emails that are sent out pretending to be Paypal to get your login credentials or pretending to be from a credit card company hoping to scam you tends to break this rule.

Don't use deceptive subject lines 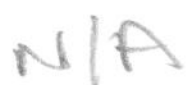

There are different degrees of deception. What is against the laws is blatant deception. An email subject that says "Open this email and you will win a new car" is clearly against the rules. An acceptable subject line is persuasive but not deceptive. Entire books are written on the topic of subject lines. I'll try to do this topic some justice in one of the last chapters of this book.

Don't use a deceptive reply-to email address

This also is the tool of a scammer. Notes that appear to come from a large company are something that we likely have all seen. Most email programs do a decent job of identifying these types of notes as spam. All newsletter services require that we use an email address that can receive mail as the displayed "reply-to" address. We will talk about the various types of email address in a future chapter.

Always provide an unsubscribe link or easy method of unsubscribing

All newsletter services have an unsubscribe link that is automatically added to the bottom of a newsletter. This helps comply with this part of the various laws we need to follow. It is important to not remove this function from newsletters that you send – and yes, this can be done.

Once a reader clicks on the unsubscribe link, they are automatically unsubscribed from your list. Although you are allowed a grace period in which to stop communicating with people who ask to be removed from your list, it is nice to have this function provided automatically.

As we will talk about in other chapters, it is a good idea to educate your readers. Many people feel that clicking on the spam button in their email program will remove them from a list. This isn't true, it just levels a complaint. Make sure that readers who want to leave know how to do that. This subject will come up again when we talk about sending reputation.

. . .

Physical Mailing Address

This last point is often one I find myself explaining to authors – especially the female ones. Most people don't want their home address appearing at the bottom of every note that they send out to readers. However, this is required by several of the legislations. I suspect this rule is directed at businesses that have a bricks and mortar location. The creators of the various law were probably not considering that some people who send out newsletters work from home or do not have a business address that is not their home.

I do not suggest that a home address is used for safety reasons. I suggest complying with this rule by obtaining a PO Box (which is quite easy and cheap in many countries) or asking your publisher or employer if their address can be used. In my 10 years of helping authors with newsletters, I have never seen anyone actually receive mail at a physical address, so to me, what the address is, is somewhat unimportant. What is important is that it is present – that it hasn't been removed.

Many authors are not aware that when they enter an address in a newsletter service profile section, this address will be visible to their readers until this is pointed out to them. Keep in mind, AN address needs to be displayed. Removing this section from the newsletter or leaving this area blank is against the legislations. Do I think you will be fined if you refuse to display your address? No. I DO feel that you need to do your best to comply with this aspect of the legislations.

One last point on this topic before we move on. The relatively new GDPR legislation out of the UK is also concerned with data storage. This is a big topic but is limited in its application to authors or to the normal activities of authors. As long as you are allowing the newsletter service to control and store all the information about members of a mailing list, they will have processes in place to be compliant with the GDPR rules. I encourage not using your personal computer to retain information about your readers. There are other aspects of the GDPR legislation that apply to your website which are out of the scope of this book.

I hope that you have a better understanding of what is needed to be compliant with the various legislations surrounding electronic communications. In the next chapter we will move on to talk about domain-based email addresses.

5

DOMAIN BASED OR PAID EMAIL ADDRESSES

As I mentioned earlier in this book, quite a few of the authors that I work with were taken aback some time ago back when they were asked to "Acknowledge the risk" of using a Gmail address as the return address by MailChimp. There have been rumblings for several years about the dangers of using a free email address - be it Gmail, Yahoo, Hotmail or something similar. Although I've always been aware that there are negative aspects to using a free email account, I've always just shoved concerns aside in favor of the cost and the convenience. I'm responsible for monitoring 27 different email accounts on a daily basis. Since there is a lovely mobile app for Gmail, loading them all onto my iPad is a really convenient thing.

When I started getting calls from authors about what MailChimp was doing, I needed to be able to come up with an explanation that non-technical people could understand. Frankly, all that MailChimp was offering was pretty complicated.

I'm sure you've all heard the expression "You're known by the company that you keep." I can explain why not to use free email addresses as your "from" or "reply to" address on an email marketing service but probably the simplest way I can describe why the free email services are bad is that saying. When an email is received, as we'll find out shortly, it is analyzed before it is actually accepted into the email program of the receiver. One of the things that is analyzed is the "from" address and the "reply to" address. Generally speaking all free email addresses are seen as a bit sketchy because of a small number of problem people. They are looked at just a little bit more closely by the receiving program. They are judged more sternly than other types of email addresses. Perhaps unfairly, but email programs need to draw a line in the sand at some point.

A domain based email address or a so-called paid email address isn't judged as harshly. Often the assumption with a domain-based email is that they're monitored more carefully by the owner. So how can I make this statement and what is a domain based email address? First of all a domain based email address has @yourdomain.com as the last half. Typically the full email address has the format of yourname@yourdomain.com. My domain based email address is Barb@Bakerviewconsulting.com. My business website domain or URL is Bakerviewconsulting.com. It is possible to set up a domain based email address at most hosting companies based on the domain of your website for free or for low-cost.

Recently Google has brought in what they call G suite. For five dollars a month you can very easily create a domain-based email address and access it just like any other Gmail address. A lot easier than some of the other options. Many people who are still working in the corporate environment have a domain based email address provided by the company that they work for. Perhaps if I worked for Nike, I could have barb@Nike.com. Most educational organizations have domain based email addresses as well. They hand them out to the staff and students. So as another example I did my university undergrad at the University of Guelph. If I had an email address there, it would likely be my name followed by the university's name, barbdrozdowich@UofGuelph.ca. I'm sure you are getting the picture.

Do I think that domain based email addresses are the be-all and end-all? No. Many people say they are more professional looking then using a Gmail or a Hotmail address. They certainly are a way of branding, as every time they are used the person who is receiving the email is reminded of the name of your domain. The other thing that's nice is that you can have numerous similar emails all with the same ending for everyone who works with you. One thing that MailChimp frowns on in terms of email addresses that newsletters are sent out to, is what they call positional emails. What's meant by that is an email address such as sales@yourdomain.com or newsletter@yourdomain.com. What is recommended is that email addresses are in the format of 'name @ domain' like the examples above.

So to finish off this discussion on emails… is it the end of the world if you decide to use a Gmail address? The answer is no. You may find that some newsletters are not being delivered, but if you are working off of a list of only a couple of thousand people that number may not be very high. MailChimp as well as several other email marketing services, have mechanisms in place to compensate. In fact if you read the help documents at MailChimp, you will find out how they can compensate for the use of free email addresses. Do I recommend that you eventually move in the direction of having a domain based email address? That answer is yes. However, I'm very aware of how many tasks an author has to carry out and how many things an author has to learn. Perhaps creating a domain based email address is something you put a little further down the list.

6

GMAIL CONCERNS

As Gmail account holders know, Gmail delivers messages to tabbed inboxes based on a complicated and ever-changing algorithm. Gmail will consider a lot of factors when determining which tab to place the email in. Many authors feel that having their newsletters land in the promotion tab of Gmail is a disaster as it will go unnoticed; others disagree. Let's look at some numbers. Some studies indicate that there is an 8 to 10% increase in open rate when newsletters show up in the primary inbox over the promotions tab (where it will typically end up.)

Keep in mind Gmail's promotions tab contains marketing and potentially promotional offers - that's what it's meant for. Although I wasn't pleased when Gmail first introduced this arrangement, I have become accustomed to it. Now I like the promotions tab as it allows for segregation of what used to be an absolute nightmare of an inbox.

In Gmail, only the subscribers can change where Gmail places your newsletter. They can do nothing and anticipate it appearing in their promotions tab. They can add your email address to their contact list and that will likely result in the newsletter appearing in their primary inbox or they can actually manually drag your newsletter from the promotions tab to the primary inbox. That action will result in the newsletter always appearing in this tab. This goes to educating your readers. Although we all have little tricks for managing our inboxes, a little education can go a long way in terms of helping!

7

THE JOURNEY OF AN EMAIL

As I've said before, many of us assume that when an email is sent it is received. Research tells us that that isn't entirely true. Have you ever considered the steps involved in sending an email? Honestly until I had to start breaking it down to explain to my authors I didn't give it a lot of thought either. I certainly have run into emails going missing over the years. I'm sure everyone has. But I hadn't really thought about the complexity of the journey of an email between being sent and being received.

Regardless of what email service or program we use to wrangle our email, it is ultimately received by an Internet Service Provider or ISP. You can think of an ISP as just a complicated computer. It has a variety of mechanisms to analyze the email coming in. Some of you may have noticed when you start up your computer in the morning that you're told your email program is "checking for mail." This process may take a while and then suddenly you're told you have X number of emails. Depending on what program you use, you may then start seeing notifications show up on your computer screen letting you know you have an email from person A, or person B, etc. Have you ever wondered why they arrive one at a time like that and why sometimes it seems to take a fair amount of time before you're told that you have email?

I used the example of checking your email first thing in the morning because, if you are like me, you wake up to 20 or 30 new emails that have arrived overnight. So the process of analyzing 20 or 30 emails is much slower than it would be for just one. This allows you to notice the time lag. When an email is sent out it carries with it information on where it comes from. - a label of sorts. The email arrives at the receiver's Internet service provider and says

"Hi I'm an email from Barb's Gmail address."

Right off the top the Internet service provider will be saying:

"Gmail, huh? This email could be a bit sketchy. I think we need to look at it a bit more carefully."

That sketchiness is a reflection on the sending server's reputation. I used the example of a Gmail address deliberately as all Gmail addresses are free addresses and are considered to be sketchy by some.

The email is then analyzed. The subject line is looked at; the content is looked at. And when I'm saying the content is looked at, not just the visible content but the code that makes up the content as well. If that code looks a bit sketchy that might be a strike against it. The Internet service provider will wonder if you've received email from Barb before. Is Barb in your contact list? Eventually the receiving Internet service provider will decide if the positives outweigh the negatives and then hopefully deliver the email. If you have a Gmail address, it needs to decide which section of your Gmail it will deliver it to - the inbox, the social tab or the promotional tab. Perhaps this email is seen as really sketchy and it's delivered to the spam or junk folder.

Bet you didn't realize it was so complicated did you?

Let's talk about 4 major factors involved in the success of this journey:

1) The Sending Server's Reputation

2) The Receiving Server's Reaction made up of:

a) Email Firewall
b) Spam Filters

8

SENDING SERVER REPUTATION

The server and domain that your emails are sent from builds up reputation over time with other email services. Because of this, the reputation of the sending server or where emails are sent from is quite important. That's why any email marketing service that you join - if they're worth their salt - will carefully guard their reputation. They will have infrastructure in place to keep track of spam complaints. They'll investigate every time they've been flagged by spam filters.

A quote from MailChimp regarding reputation:

> "We work hard to maintain a great sending reputation by following best practices and giving our users the tools they need to stay compliant with anti-spam laws. When you send a campaign, our automated abuse prevention system, Omnivore, scans your campaign and analyzes addresses that could affect the delivery of your campaign. These measures help protect your sending reputation as well as ours, thereby keeping your campaigns out of spam filters."

There is a saying that a company is only as good as its weakest link. I've helped several authors who have had warning notes from MailChimp or whichever service they're using. Although these notes are a point of stress, as someone who is also a user of an email marketing service, I'm happy that they are taking preventative measures against points of concern. In my experience, it's common for authors who don't understand what best practices are, to run into problems. Once best practices are explained, most people that I work with understand how to do things properly.

9

RECEIVING SERVERS

As we've already mentioned, in order for your email to get you to your readers, it needs to be scanned by the receiving server, or email program. As one would expect different servers, and different email programs all have different sets of rules. Some are quite lax, and some are very aggressive in their actions. Quite honestly if you are following best practices, your email or newsletter may get delayed a bit for further examination, but will likely get to the recipient.

There are two main mechanisms serving as monitors and gatekeepers for emails - **Email Firewalls** and **Email Spam Filters**.

A) Email Firewalls

All email goes through two different kinds of mechanisms before it hits your inbox. It has to pass through a spam filter after it passes through an email firewall. All Internet service providers have these two mechanisms but there is variation amongst what type is used.

. . .

Let's talk about email firewalls first.

An email firewall will look at all incoming email as well as outgoing email and collect information about it. Not all firewalls are identical but what is common amongst them is that they monitor the behavior of people sending email and they communicate with one another.

Think of them as the neighborhood gossip. When the recipient of one of your emails clicks on that junk or spam button, the firewall is the one to pass on that message. I'm sure you can picture it. The firewall sends out a message to all its friends letting them know that your email just got declared spam. And just like that everybody's looking at you funny…

If emails are declared spam or junk often enough your sending reputation will be damaged. Firewalls can blacklist problems senders. In order to maintain your sending reputation you want to avoid being flagged by the email firewall. The easiest way you can do this is to educate the receivers of your newsletter and let them know how to unsubscribe. Many authors actually advise putting the unsubscribe button or link at the top of the note. Honestly, the last thing you want is a whole bunch of receivers damaging your reputation by using the spam or junk button. If you are using an email marketing service not only will you get in trouble, you may actually be asked to leave. That's not something that you want happening.

B) Spam Filters

Let's move on to spam filters.

Spam filters are programs that will scan all email to determine whether it should be delivered or not. These filters use a variety of criteria to judge incoming email. Unlike is commonly reported there isn't any one saying or "spam word" that will stop email from being delivered. All spam filters will create what's called a spam score based on a number of different criteria. The higher the score the less likely the email is to be delivered.

Spam filters are programs that are getting better and better at screening email. In past years, it was easy to get beyond a spam filter because they wouldn't scan much more than the subject line. They might take a glance at the content, but they were fairly easy to fool. Today's spam filters are much more sophisticated.

So if we know this much about spam filters how do we avoid being tagged by them?

There isn't a one-size-fits-all set of instructions as every spam filter is a little bit different. Because of this we can talk about best practices rather than no-fail guidelines.

Let's look at 3 areas that are scrutinized by spam filters:

1) Metadata

Metadata, by definition is small pieces of information. So when we talk about the metadata in an email or a newsletter we're talking about small things not big things. For example spam filters are more likely to object to an email if it is only addressed to an email address and not the person's first name. Because of this I suggest that you collect at least the first name of all of your subscribers. When you send out newsletters you allow your email marketing system to address each note to the person's first name.

Spam filters will also look to see if you are already on your recipient's contact list. And as I've mentioned before the free email addresses are viewed as much more sketchy than domain based addresses. So if an email is coming in from a free email address hopefully you will be on the person's contact list in order to get a somewhat free pass.

Lastly emails or newsletters coming in from email marketing services will have embedded in them a form of authentication to help it be delivered, or to help it be seen as valid.

2) Content and Format

Spam filters will look at the content and the format that is used of any email that tries to pass them. Years ago spammers would get emails through spam filters by putting their message on an image and including little else in their message. The spam filter couldn't read the image, and couldn't find anything objectionable in the text so it was passed. Although spam filters have become increasingly sophisticated they still can't read pictures. Keep that in mind if you are thinking about sending a newsletter with a picture and very little text. It could potentially be problematic.

Today's spam filters tend to look at things like the ratio of pictures to text and make a judgment. Beyond that spam filters will also look at the format of the message and will look at all of the links in the message to see if they are valid. It's fairly common knowledge that spammers use link shorteners to disguise where the links are sending

people. That makes the use of link shorteners especially Bit.ly links, not a good practice. Simply take the full hyperlink and embed it into the text of the newsletter. Other things to avoid in terms of content are strings of all capital letters - in the subject line as well as in the body text, obvious spam phrases such as "once-in-a-lifetime opportunity," excessive exclamation points, excessive colored font, and what I'll call weird text - creating words using letters and numbers. Many experts will like you to believe that there is a massive list of "spam words" and if you avoid them, you will be fine. This simply isn't true.

3) Code

Along with the obvious content of an email or newsletter, the spam filter will scan the HTML code. This is something that you may not actually see in a newsletter or an email, but it is the behind-the-scenes creating of bolded text and other formatting. One of the most common problems when creating a newsletter is when people copy and paste from Word (or other word processing programs) into the newsletter template. That action can bring all sorts of background code with it. Email spam filters consider this excessive code a possible strike against you. One of the actions that we'll talk about in the last section of this book is the recommendation to either create your email within the service that you use, or pass material from Word through a text editor to get rid of the excessive code. We'll talk about this more in a future chapter.

Looking at the big picture, you want to make sure that people have opted into your list, your note is personalized, it fits within industry standards, you are using content or text to catch attention but not in a bad way, the domain or the IP address that the newsletters are sent from has a good reputation and there aren't any obvious red flags.

So the question is how do you know if you have a problem? Is it always obvious? No, it isn't always obvious. Until you have a track record it is difficult to read your stats properly. When you are first starting out with a newsletter it's difficult to determine how to get your readers to respond and how to work the system properly. It's also difficult to determine if there are any problems - especially if you don't understand how to read the analytics.

10

WHAT ARE EXAMPLES OF EMAIL MARKETING SERVICES AND WHAT TO LOOK FOR IN AN EMAIL MARKETING SERVICE?

There is a huge number of email marketing services. The one we will focus on in this book is Mailerlite. There are lots of others to choose from, some good and some not as good. Some very simple and some that are very complicated. Some of the more common examples are:

- Constant Contact
- AWeber
- ConvertKit
- GetResponse
- CampaignMonitor
- ActiveCampaign
- IContact
- Campaigner
- Pinpointe
- Benchmark email
- VerticalResponse
- Mad Mimi
- Infusionsoft
- 1PointMail

. . .

And the list goes on.

Since there are so many choices, let's talk about what to look for in a service.

1) Visual Editor. The last thing most authors want to do is figure out how to code a newsletter, so the presence of a visual editing system is very important. Typically, this will allow the user to drag and drop a picture, type in some text and immediately get a general idea of what their subscribers will see in their newsletter. Most authors don't have any interest in dealing with HTML or CSS code, and would rather rely on the Email Marketing Service to handle that part of the newsletter. In this day and age one would assume that all services use a visual editor. That isn't true and not all visual editors are created equal.

2) Integration with your website or blog - Although it seems like an obvious point, you want to make sure that you choose an Email Marketing Service that easily integrates with your website or blog to allow for a seamless collection of emails for your mailing list. Honestly one of the main reasons why I chose Mailerlite was because of how straight-forward it was to connect my blog to my Mailerlite account. Several years have passed and there are several more choices that are now fairly easy. This may not be a concern of yours if you have a website developer handling that type of activity, but if you are a do-it-yourselfer this might be a very important consideration.

3) Analytics and Reports - Although I'm quite the stats geek, I realize I don't share that interest with most authors. Most authors are generally only concerned with open rates and click through rates. Information such as are your emails being opened on a mobile device, how many are being forwarded on to friends, and what country are your subscribers from, are interesting pieces of information that you can leverage. Not all analytics are created equal. Make sure that you choose a service that doesn't require an advanced degree to understand the analytics.

4) **Autoresponders** - Once you get beyond the initial collection of information, you may want a service that allows you to automate the process of sending out some newsletters. Experts suggest that newcomers to your mailing list are welcomed with a small series of notes. This is an example of autoresponders. In fact autoresponders can become quite complicated. Not all services are set up to provide an autoresponder sequence, and not all autoresponder systems are as easy to navigate as others.

5) Anti-spam legislation compliance - Whenever we send out newsletters we need to be aware that we need to be compliant with the anti-spam laws of our country. Most civilized countries have anti-spam legislation. Since most of the Email Marketing Services originate from the US, most will claim to be CAN-SPAM compliant as that's the name of the American legislation. The main aspect we are concerned with in this section is the ability for readers to unsubscribe. Most anti-spam legislation sets out time periods during which people can be expected to be removed from lists. What most Email Marketing Services do for you is automatically remove names when the unsubscribe link is clicked. This allows you to remain compliant. The main point here is that using a service as opposed to using your Gmail account will help you remain compliant.

6) **List segmentation** -There are a number of reasons why you would want to segment your list. As we discussed in a previous book from this collection, it's not uncommon for authors to allow their audience to choose which frequency of newsletter they get. In many cases the audi-

ence segments themselves when they sign up. It's also handy to be able to send a past newsletter to everyone who has subscribed since the previous one. These are common examples of segmentation that you may wish to take advantage of. As you progress you may wish to do things like send a note to everyone who clicked on a particular link in your previous note, or send a note to everyone who lives in a particular country. These should be fairly easy activities with an email marketing service.

One aspect that isn’t listed above is difficulty level. If you are just starting out or aren’t very technical, look for a service that is praised for it’s ease of use. However, I don’t recommend using a service just because it is easy but is lacking in some of the above or choosing a service that is easy but doesn’t have very good delivery stats.

11

WHY SHOULD YOU CHOOSE AN EMAIL MARKETING SERVICE?

Now that we have talked about examples of email marketing services and what features to look for when choosing a service, let's talk about why you should choose to use a service.

Formatting - In this technical age, expectations can be high. We are expected to produce a polished, entertaining and attractive newsletter to our readers. As I'm sure you know, email looks different on various different email programs. When we send out a newsletter, we may refer to it as an email, but it is in fact more than that. It is a combination of text and pictures and hyperlinks. It is optimized for delivery to most email providers. In fact the information that we include in a newsletter has special code to style it and make it look nice. This isn't something that most email programs are capable of doing. The email that comes from an Email Marketing Service has been designed to look good on mobile devices, tablets, as well as desktops. As we know, more and more email is read on phones.

. . .

List Management - Gone are the days when we keep a list of emails on a spreadsheet on the computer. We no longer copy and paste a massive list of email addresses from email to email. Not only does it make it difficult to deal with the anti-spam legislation requirement, but quite frankly, most determined authors can have lists numbering in the tens of thousands. A service is needed to help manage that list. As I said in the last section, the more you progress with newsletters the nicer it is to be able to send specialized notes to certain segments of your list. This is just not possible when you use an Excel spreadsheet.

Legalities - We've mentioned the legalities before, and this subject will continue to come up. Frankly being found in contravention of some of the anti-spam legislation can result in fines of thousands of dollars if not more. If nothing else, it is nice to have a service that will keep track of unsubscribes, so if challenged this service can provide proof of adherence with legislation.

A/B Testing - One interesting feature of most email marketing services is the ability to send out two different versions of a newsletter - something that's called A/B testing. It's possible to test two different subject lines to see how they resonate with your audience. Clearly if you are just starting out and only have 10 names on your list this may not be something that you are interested in, but as you progress it is a cool feature to use.

Analytics and Statistics - I like numbers; I like using numbers to prove things. I like being able to tell how many people open my newsletters. If I'm offering a free book to my subscribers, I like to know how many people took me up on my offer. These pieces of information help me understand how I'm resonating with my audience. Regardless of what your friends say, Gmail does not give you stats. It cannot tell you how many notes are opened and how many links are clicked on. No idea of how successful your hard work of creating a newsletter is. Only an email marketing service will do this for you.

12

WHAT ARE OPEN AND CLICK-THROUGH RATES AND WHY ARE THEY IMPORTANT?

Open rates and click through rates are two of the most common stats that are paid attention to on newsletters. They are considered to measure your readers engagements with your newsletters. Let's talk about some definitions:

Open rates - The open rate is typically expressed as a percentage. This number will tell you how many successfully delivered campaigns are opened by your readers.

Click rates (are also called click through rates) - This number is also expressed as a percentage. Typically this number refers to how many successfully delivered campaigns received at least one click.

Both open rates and click through rates are numbers that are to be taken with a grain of salt. One of the main reasons for this is most email marketing services will embed a tiny image in the newsletter to help determine open rates. As we've discussed before, an email that is viewed in a preview pane won't always be counted as an open. Again some numbers - as many as 84% of all email readers will view email in a preview pane set up. An email that is opened without loading the images won't be counted as an open. Lastly an email opened on many mobile devices doesn't record properly as an open. Many email marketing services will try to adjust the open rate by using the click rate to try and present more accurate numbers but as you can see calculating statistics is a grey area - not necessarily black or white.

Keep in mind that the open rate will not be equal to the delivery rate. As we've discussed previously, it is unlikely that 100% of your newsletters will actually be delivered. Emails can bounce for various reasons. We are hoping that by using an email marketing service a really large percentage of our newsletters will be delivered - in fact, we're looking for in excess of 97% or 98% of them. Just as an aside, most email marketing services will let you know their average delivery rate. They should publicize it somewhere.

So why are we focusing on open rates and not delivery rates. I suppose you can say that we will do everything we can to get a high delivery rate, but the open rate will depend on human action. Your readers need to decide whether or not to open a newsletter from you based on who it's from and the subject line and little else in many cases. It's true people that have access to an email program that gives them a preview pane and therefore may have access to more of the content than just the subject line, but many will make an open decision based on not very much. Experts will say if you have a strong open rate, it usually means that your subject line resonates with your readers and if your click rate or click through rate is good the message content resonates with your readers.

Most of the email marketing services will provide benchmarks. As you saw in the previous book of this collection, when I walked you through the process of opening a Mailerlite account, one of the pieces of information that I needed to give them was the industry. They use that to supply some benchmark numbers. In my experience those benchmark numbers are fairly low as they are based on averages over a large number of accounts. What I suggest doing is ignoring the benchmarks and paying attention to your own track records. This is difficult to do when you're first starting out but as you go along you will get an idea of how your audience tends to react to your newsletters. Certainly pay attention to any distinctly different numbers that suddenly appear.

Let's talk about some of the common strategies that can be used to improve open rates.

1) Subject line - I will spend more time on the subject line in the last book of this collection, but as I mentioned in the previous section, your readers, generally speaking, get two pieces of information to help them determine whether or not to open your newsletter or your email - the email address and who the newsletter is from along with your subject line. According to the legalities your subject line should be representative of the content of your newsletter. So using a subject line like "Open this newsletter to get your free car" is not a good plan. Likewise a non-informative subject line, while not against the various anti-spam laws, won't necessarily encourage the opening of the note or newsletter. Using a subject line of "Newsletter #1" followed by Newsletter #2 and so on may be a helpful way of keeping track of your newsletters but it doesn't give any information about the content to your readers. Likewise subject lines that are named after the month or the season are equally unhelpful. So try something different from "Your January newsletter" or "Spring News."

As we've discussed before most of the email marketing services provide you with the ability to test subject lines. There are also external services or websites that will help you test subject lines. We'll talk about these in the last book of this collection. But as I said before, creating a sense of urgency or having your readers eagerly anticipate your newsletter is one of the best things that you can do and typically that is done by having great content.

2) Segment your list - Remember, segmenting your list means breaking up your list into functional pieces. It means sending emails to people based on what country they live in, what links they clicked on in the previous newsletter, or in fact what interests they selected when they originally signed up for your newsletter if you offered that possibility. Targeted emails are always considered to be of higher value to the reader than just a generalized email blast. Think about your list and what you can do with your group of readers to create more targeted communication.

3) Frequency - How often do you send out newsletters? And a second question: How do you determine how often to send out newsletters? A well-accepted fact in the industry, is that email sent out too frequently won't to be opened at the same rate or with the same level of enthusiasm. There are exceptions certainly. If you have an upcoming release and you're gradually feeding information to your readers, - a sneak peak at the front cover of the book, some little tidbits of information about the storyline and so on, can be considered valuable content by your readers. In fact it can be content that is eagerly anticipated. However, if your newsletters are boring, people will stop opening them. There are experts out there that insist newsletters are sent out on a regular schedule. Yet it should be noted that these experts don't tend to give you any advice about what to say in order for that newsletter to be eagerly read.

I tend to follow the rule of thumb that if you don't have anything of interest to say, don't send out a newsletter. However there are strategies for sending out content when you have nothing to share and we'll talk about them in more depth in the last book of this collection. There are activities like giving away a book that you've enjoyed reading, It might cost three or four dollars on Amazon but that small amount of money might help endear you to your readers as you're not just talking about yourself.

Let's talk about how to improve click through rates.

As I said above, click through rates or click rates are considered to be an indication of engagements with your newsletter. If you provide a variety of sources of information that you're sharing with your readers and they engage with that content, you have created a valuable resource for them.

1) Make links clear - As we've all been told in our corporate life, don't click on links in an email where you don't know the source. Common Internet security 101. If you have a sentence in your newsletter that says for "more information click here," that phrase "click here" might actually discourage your readers from clicking. Try changing the words. As an example you can say for more information on this subject I'm going to send you to the blog post on my blog to read more about this subject. You can hyperlink the phrase "read more." Is this any different from just saying click here? It is to a certain extent. By using a more robust sentence you are explaining to your readers where they will end up going if they click on the link. They still have to trust you, but sometimes using more words will make them feel more comfortable.

Another example, if we are talking about sending somebody to purchase a book, instead of saying "buy here" and have the "buy here" phrase hyperlinked to wherever your book is available, why not say my book is available on Amazon, Barnes & Noble, iTunes and Kobo with each of the words hyperlinked to the buy page on that particular retailer. Again, a little bit more information is a little bit more comforting to the reader. One last comment: make the links visible. Choose a color that will stand out, underline them. Don't make your readers guess where the links are by hovering their mouse around looking for a color change

2) More links - If you put all your eggs in one basket…you know the saying. Instead of creating a newsletter that has only one or two hyperlinks or places to click, why not create a newsletter that supplies lots of information to your readers. That way you can appeal to different readers in different ways. If all you put in your newsletter is buy links, your reader may get turned off. If you offer a selection of purchase links, also provide links to points of information. Don't make them feel that all you want them to do is buy. Don't just treat them like a wallet. A last note about links that we talked about when talking about Mailer-lite - make sure you go through the process to check all of your links before you send your newsletter out and as we've suggested before, don't use shortened links; embed the full length link.

3) Testing your content - One of the most common pieces of information from marketing experts is to A/B test your campaigns. We'll discuss this in an upcoming chapter.

13

EMAIL PROGRAMS

While researching for this book, I decided to learn more about email programs. I personally have a Mac and have always used MacMail. I am an addicted Gmail user, so I'm very familiar with both programs/platforms. I might grumble at times, but not enough to change my work processes and use something else. When I was in the corporate environment, I was typically given access to Outlook for email handling. At the time, I mastered the use of Outlook and didn't really complain.

How many email programs are there out there? Throughout my research, I was continually finding references to emails read on a program or app that had a preview pane, and programs that didn't load pictures by default.

I was amazed at the results. Here's a short list of the more popular programs/apps according to several sources:

- Gmail
- Microsoft Outlook
- Windows Live Mail
- Mozilla Thunderbird

- Mac Mail
- Microsoft Entourage
- Android native email client
- Android Gmail app
- Android Yahoo Mail app
- iOS Mail app
- iOS Gmail app
- iOS Yahoo Mail app
- Zoho mail
- BoltMail
- HotMail
- YahooMail
- Opera
- Mailbird
- Pegasus Mail
- IncrediMail
- Mail for Windows
- Mulberry
- Foxmail
- DreamMail
- Alpine
- Sylpheed
- i.Scribe
- Spark
- Canary Mail
- Nylas Mail Basic
- Polymail
- Mozilla SeaMonkey
- Roundcube

How many do you recognize on the list? You'll notice that some are email programs - such as Mac Mail, some are apps for mobile devices such as iOS Gmail app and many are Webmail applications or something that is signed into like a website. In fact a quick search turned up 58 different programs or apps. Clearly, some are more popular than others, but I had no idea that there were so many choices available.

In fact, one of the articles I read (Email Client Market Share and Popularity - Jan 2017) listed the top 10 email clients by popularity with the top 5 being:

- Apple iPhone - 31% of market share
- Gmail - 20% of market share
- Apple iPad - 12% of market share
- Google Android - 8% of market share
- Apple Mail - 7% of market share

The one thing that jumps out at me from this list is that 3 of the top 5 are mobile apps. This confirms the suggestions that many people read their email on a mobile device.

As I was searching programs and apps to add to my list, many of the listings had screenshots of what the interface looks like. Many of the choices have a preview functionality of one sort or another. Many of the non-mobile choices had a full preview pane showing as much as the first paragraph of the email. Most of the mobile apps, like the typical Gmail interface, show a short preview of information. The number of characters that are visible vary from app to app, but typically range from a high of 140 to a low of 35 characters.

At this point, I would encourage you to study the display for the various ways **you** access email. If you are like me, you just take for granted what's there and don't really study it; it's normal. Count the number of characters you see or count the number of lines you see. If you look closely, you'll see that the display is cut off at the end of the character count - which may or may not result in an attractive display. Although the mobile apps are pretty rigid in their character count, you might be able to see the mail programs viewed on a desktop or laptop screen are responsive to the width of the window they are viewed in.

What's the takeaway from all this information? I think it is several fold. First of all, the vast majority of our newsletter receivers will have access to more than just sender name/email address and subject line to make a decision of whether or not to read more. Secondly, as I've read in many places, many people have access to an email program that offers a preview pane type of preview of an email/newsletter. Thirdly, the access to a preview pane may skew the ability to monitor what Email Marketing Services call Open Rates.

Let's expand a bit on some of this information. As we discuss in this book, using all 150 or so characters in the subject line is not necessarily a good thing. With most mobile devices only showing on average 50 characters, and desktop devices showing maybe 75 characters of the subject line, we want to front-load and keep short, the subject line. However, with many mobile devices seeing at least some of the first part of the text of your newsletter, you want to take advantage of that also. Make your first sentence powerful. Give them a reason to read further!

To take advantage of the apparently large number of folks who have access to a preview pane, we want to provide great content at the beginning of our newsletters and give them a reason to continue to scroll in the preview pane.

One of the complaints that is quite common, is that newsletters that are viewed in a Preview Pane type of functionality are often not counted as opens. Newsletter services admit that it counts opens by embedding a tiny picture in the note and then counts the note as opened when the little picture is loaded - which commonly doesn't occur in a preview pane functionality. Also, the email programs that don't automatically load images (which also is apparently common) won't load the little picture and count the email as an open. Newsletter services compensate by using information from clicks. In other words, whether a newsletter is registered as an open or not may depend on clicking. If something is clicked on in the note, it will be counted as an open but if nothing is clicked on, it is seen as unopened. But what about the folks that use a preview pane, don't load pictures and don't click on any links? They may be smiling and nodding as they read, but if you don't supply a link they want to click on, nothing!

Email Marketing Services use a variety of methods to collect their stats. Some embed little graphics; some have more complicated methods. Some will say that the pictures don't need to be loaded to count as an open, that their monitoring system is more sophisticated than that. Ultimately, stats are just stats; they are meant to be an indication of action, not meant as an absolute number. In fact, one source suggested that most open rates are around 30% underrepresented. So, if you see an open rate of 45% for a newsletter, it is likely more like 75%. And that may be true.

You are probably saying to yourself. My newsletters are always interesting, front-loaded and full of links, something for everyone! And I'm sure you are correct.

I send out a lot of technical help information in my newsletters - tips and tricks for tasks authors have difficulty with. Just before Christmas, I ran into an author at an author meet and greet who mentioned that she has all my newsletters saved in a file in her email program and is hoping to have the time to study them soon. She's been dealing with the death of a parent, and has had other things occupying her time for the last year or so. She'll read them when she's ready. She hasn't opened them yet, though…

As I'm sure I've mentioned, I'm Canadian. My Kindle app is connected to my Amazon.ca account. You see, I read romance and some of what I read isn't really appropriate for the younger members of my family. I figured out early on that Kindle doesn't provide a mechanism to block certain content. Anyone who uses an app or device attached to an account has access to it all. So, I left the family Kindle apps and devices attached to the Amazon.com account and opened myself up an Amazon.ca account and attached the Kindle app on my iPad to that account. It was too complicated to open a second Amazon.com account. I needed a second credit card and a second address, etc. The Amazon.ca account was easy to do.

The point of this story is that when I buy a book to read, I have to buy it from Amazon.ca to read it on my Kindle app. The vast majority of newsletters I get about books will have a buy link for Amazon.com and perhaps Amazon.co.uk but very rarely do authors either use universal links or offer direct links to Amazon.ca (or other minor Amazon choices) Because of this, I've gotten into the habit of independently searching on Amazon.ca for any book that I'm interested in from a newsletter and buying it directly. I rarely click on links in a newsletter because they don't lead to a site that I can buy from.

I am a voracious reader who views author newsletters on MacMail, which has a preview pane, and I don't typically click on links in the newsletter. Do I count? I buy books and I respond to newsletters in my own way, but likely my actions don't register anywhere.

Many of the current Mailing List experts will suggest a form of Mailing list hygiene. They suggest periodically removing folks from your list who don't engage. In other words, remove everyone who hasn't opened a newsletter in a determined period of time. The reasoning is - why pay for folks who aren't engaging? I guess that's why I'm periodically removed from mailing lists, sadly.

Before you follow the advice of the experts and carry out regular mailing list hygiene, look at your stats and look at your content. Where do your subscribers live? If you are providing buy links for only Amazon.com, yet the vast majority of your audience doesn't live in the US, are you providing them something to click on that works for their needs? Do you only send out notes that talk about time sensitive information like sales, or do you send out information, like me, that can be put away and read at a more appropriate time for the reader?

I always say that knowledge is power. Use this information, as well as information that you can gather about your readers, and perhaps make different choices than what the experts suggest.

14

STRATEGIES TO IMPROVE DELIVERABILITY

In this section we're going to talk about some basic, and I like to think, common sense strategies to improve deliverability of your emails or newsletters.

1) Educate your readers

You'll notice I put this piece of advice as the first one. In all the reading that I've done, subscribers to a mailing list are treated or talked about in a variety of different ways. A lot of the experts in the field feel readers are a skittish bunch. They give pieces of information like "Get your subscribers to sign up using a Lead Generation advertisement on Facebook - it's fast! They aren't asked for much information and they don't have the chance to have a second thought." Many experts will suggest that you only ask your subscribers for their email address. They say: "Don't worry about their first or last name or do any kind of questioning when they're signing up. It might confuse them. It will give them a chance to back away." I don't disagree to a certain extent. But honestly we want to have subscribers on our mailing list who want to be there; who are interested in our work or what we have to say, and obviously we want them to buy some of our books.

I have a different view of subscribers than many. I see them as friends who want to learn what I have to teach and then gain the ability to reproduce those lessons. The vast majority of my audience are either authors or bloggers, and the information that I share in the blogs that I write is information they need, activities they need to learn to sell their own books, or to manage their own blogs.

So, I want to be clear with my subscribers what they are going to get from me and how often they are going to get it. I follow the old saying "prevention is better than the cure." I want somebody to realize what I'm going to send, before I send it. If this isn't something that they're interested in I encourage them to unsubscribe. I welcome all my subscribers to my lists with a welcome note, and I encourage them to include my email address or my return address in their contacts list which, as I've mentioned, will help my newsletters get delivered. I let them know how they can remove themselves from my list. And in fact, all of my lists are double opt in. In other words, somebody enters an email address and a name in one place and then they have to click on a button in an email to confirm sign up. Is it easier to get large numbers of people on your mailing list if you only do a single option? Absolutely. I choose not to do that because at this point, we are back to talking about hoarding, not engaging with readers.

The last point for this section is to make sure that you communicate regularly and consistently with your mailing list. As we've talked about in previous sections, lists older than six months are considered to be somewhat stale. People change email address providers; people move jobs. So as you communicate with your readers, ask them questions and educate them. For your own peace of mind make sure that they understand how they can unsubscribe from your list, and make sure they know how to update their own preferences so that they can give you their new email address.

2) Insist on Double Opt-in

We touched on double opt-in in the previous point. I can't stress this enough. Double opt-in will allow your subscribers to confirm their intent. It will also allow your email marketing service to have record of the fact that your subscriber double opted-in if any concerns are raised. The double opt-in process also protects your lists from spambots, as the spambots won't complete the process by clicking on the confirmation note.

I have heard from many authors that are frustrated with the double opt-in process. There are a number of problems that authors need to field when using this process. The first and foremost is that most email marketing services won't allow an email address to be subscribed to more than once. This is a handy safeguard that prevents duplication. However handy it is, most sign-up forms will allow somebody to enter an email address and other information, and then return a standard confirmation message. If the message is the default one, the confirmation note is often not very helpful. Even most custom messages will typically direct subscribers to look at their inbox for a confirmation note. It won't say anything about the fact that if you have already subscribed you won't get a note. I've witnessed people trying time after time after time to sign up for mailing lists, frustrated that they aren't getting a confirmation note, commonly claiming the sign up form is broken. It isn't; it's working as it's supposed to, but obviously subscribers can forget which lists that they've signed up for. The other problem that can happen is that the confirmation note goes to spam. We always hope that that doesn't happen right off the bat. It sets a bad precedent. Add to that some people's email service providers will automatically cull email that is considered to be spam and they never actually see it.

One of the best sign-up systems that I've seen in a long time had a very clear sign up form, and an excellent confirmation note. In other words as soon as I clicked on the submit button, a message appeared on my screen that did a number of things. First of all it let me know that I was going to be looking for a confirmation note in the inbox of my email program; it let me know what email address the note would be coming from so that I could add that to my contact list. And lastly it told me that the note could take up to 10 minutes to arrive in my inbox, and to make sure that I checked my spam or junk folders if it didn't arrive promptly.

Although I agree not everybody reads and follows instructions, this author did her best to help me understand what was going to be happening.

One last note for this section. Just because you have friends who will likely be interested in your writing, doesn't mean you should automatically add them to your mailing list. It's perfectly acceptable to email friends and offer them the link to sign up, but don't assume.

3) Send your note from a newsletter service provider

This is an obvious point as this whole collection is talking about email marketing services and the proper way to send newsletters to our readers, or the optimum way to send newsletters to our readers. But you want to set a precedent right from the beginning. You are a professional running a business and acting in a professional manner. Using a newsletter service provider will communicate to your recipients that you're conducting yourself in a professional manner, and it will do everything in its power to keep your notes from ending up in spam folders

4) Send all notes with authentication

There are two different kinds of authentication that your newsletter can be sent with. The first one is the salutation. All email marketing services will allow you to send newsletters addressed at least to the first name of the person whose email address the note is going to, that is, if you collected the name. As we've talked about in previous sections, addressing an email or a newsletter to the person by name sends a signal to the recipient's email provider that you know this person - that you belong. Secondly, email marketing services have technical ways to authenticate or verify emails that normal email providers don't have access to. It's like an invisible ink stamp on your email that can only be read by the recipient's email program but isn't actually visible to your readers.

5) Carefully choose your subject line

We are going to talk about the topic of subject lines twice in this collection. In this section, we'll be talking about subject lines with respect to deliverability. In the last book of the collection we'll talk about some theories about creating the most attractive subject line.

Keep in mind, the subject line and the email address that the newsletter is from are possibly the only things that your recipients see. And they make a decision to open your newsletter based on those two pieces of information. I do realize that some people have an email program that shows them a preview pane of some sort and they may be able to scroll through more of your email, but we can not assume who has access to this technology.

Email programs are responsive. If a recipient repeatedly deletes an email from you without reading it, your deliverability will start to decrease. (You'll remember that we discussed the neighborhood gossip aka the Email Firewall.) Not necessarily your overall delivery but your delivery to this person, the email program will get the message that this person doesn't want to see emails from you and will send them directly to the spam or a junk folder or after a while perhaps, bounce them back to the sender.

I've mentioned a few common sense things that you want to take note of in terms of the subject line. These are things like using all capital letters, multiple exclamation points, excessive punctuation, etc. Not many people do things like that anymore but it is worth pointing out the obvious. The other obvious ploys that used to be fairly common were to put "re:" or "fwd:" at the beginning of the subject line trying to fool the recipient that your newsletter is a response to an email from them or that your email is has been forwarded from one of their friends. Again it's not something that's commonly done anymore but if it's advice you've been given, that's not good advice.

. . .

We'll spend more time in the next book of this collection on subject lines and content of your actual email but an excellent piece of advice that I read when researching this book is that you want your email to create a sense of urgency. You want your readers to eagerly anticipate the arrival of your email or newsletter.

6) Content

Again, like the previous section we'll talk more about the actual content in the next book of this collection but what we're talking about here is deliverability with respect to content. At the beginning of this chapter I mentioned that an old-school trick of spammers was to put their content in an image because the spam filters couldn't read images. And the email looked rather innocuous, being made up of just one image perhaps. The spam filters have gotten more sophisticated, however, the last thing that you want to do is send out a newsletter with only one image. Modern spam filters are more about reputation then content, but sending out a newsletter like that is simply asking for trouble. What you do want to do is to have a note that has an appropriate ratio of images to text. Experts say that the human brain can absorb information in an image much faster than it can a representative amount of text. And, let's face it, the images make the newsletter more visually attractive.

The last note I'll include is to remind you that a really large number of email programs don't automatically load pictures into the email. The default state is to require the recipient to click on a button in order to see the pictures. So, although pictures make a newsletter more attractive, make sure that you make use of the alt text field to give readers something to see if they can't or choose not to load the images.

. . .

7) URL Shorteners

The use of URL shorteners is also a common trick used by spammers. They use shorteners to hide the actual identity of the URL that they're linking to. Remember that when an email is scanned by a recipient they will see the visual content as well as the background code which the readers don't see. So it is advisable to embed the full length URL into your newsletter. Don't show the whole long ugly hyperlink. You can embed it to make it look nicer, yet the spam filters can read it and realize that you're not trying to hide the identity of a sketchy website.

The last point I'll make in this section is to make sure that you use an attractive 'Call to Action.' Many people will put Calls to Action in images and as you realized in the previous section that sometimes the images don't load. You want to make sure that you will describe in advance what's going to happen once they click on a particular link. Are they going to download an item and are they going to be taken to another website?

8) Unsubscribe

As we've mentioned before, make it easy to unsubscribe. In fact it seems to becoming more of a fashion to include the unsubscribe button right up front near the beginning of the newsletter. This seems to be especially common with the first email that is sent as part of a welcome package. Remember, if people are frustrated and don't want to get your newsletter any longer, they need to easily find an unsubscribe button or they are quite likely to click on the spam or junk button on their email program. We know this doesn't remove them from the list but what it does is damage your sending reputation.

The main reason that you don't want people on your list who don't want to be there is not only are you potentially paying for those people to be on your list but their lack of participation will reflect badly on the stats of your newsletter and your perception by email firewalls.

. . .

9) Sending emails to low open rate lists

If you remember back when I was talking about email firewalls I compared them to the neighborhood gossip. If you send out a bunch of newsletters to a bunch of people who don't open the emails, or maybe they just ignore the email or they click on delete, the firewalls will talk. They communicate with one another about how your readers are not engaged with your content. This goes towards your sending reputation.

As we talked about in the previous point not only are you potentially paying for these people to be on your list but they can ultimately be harmful to your ability to successfully send notes out. There are two things you can do about this. Many authors periodically send what I'll call a "re-engagement campaign" to readers that haven't opened an email in some period of time - let's say a year. Frequently that campaign has the title of "Checking to see if you are still interested in hearing from me." This provides readers a graceful out. Other experts in the field encourage mailing list hygiene to be carried out periodically. Mailing list hygiene is going through your list and simply removing people who haven't engaged with you in a certain period of time. Most email marketing services will help you do this through their segmentation function. As we've discussed before, I don't recommend this.

I'm not sure if there is a correct answer to this but I do know there's no point paying for people who are really showing by their actions that they aren't interested in being on your last. The damage to your sending reputation is one thing, the financial concern is another. I suggest finding a method of cleaning up your list every so often that works with your personality and your audience and keep with it. However, as I write this, I want you to be aware that it may be difficult to determine who isn't engaging with your notes unless you help your readers engage by providing appropriate content.

10) Ask subscribers to white list you

We mentioned this back in the in the very first point about your subscribers being educated, but it's worth repeating in isolation. Not only do you want your readers educated on a variety of subjects, but also your newsletters are much more likely to be received if they add to your email address to their contact list. That's what's meant as white listing.

11) Offer both HTML and text version of all newsletters

I know it's difficult to envision how other people read their emails. I'm used to seeing my own email program. To me what I use is normal. In reality there are many different email programs available for use and they all look different. As I've mentioned before with respect to pictures, some email programs in order to save space or to increase efficiency, default to no images being shown in emails. In the same fashion some email programs prefer an HTML version of the email and some prefer a plain text version. If you provide both, your newsletter is more likely to be delivered to all email programs.

12) Create your content within your email marketing services program editor

One of the worst things that you can do when creating a newsletter is to create that newsletter in Word and copy and paste it over to the template in your email marketing service. Most authors are pretty comfortable working in Word. When faced with the idea of creating a newsletter most of us will open a fresh Word document and start typing. I understand that comfort. If this is how you're going to create your newsletters, you will need to pass the content (ie. the text) through a TextEdit program before pasting it into the forming newsletter. The most common TextEdit program for the PC is Notepad, and the Mac has a program called TextEdit. This will remove the extra HTML coding that could be seen as sketchy to Spam Filters.

. . .

13) Don't be fooled into accepting 3rd party lists - or at least be very wary of accepting them. Most authors are aware that they shouldn't be purchasing sketchy lists from marketing services. Some lists created by group marketing efforts can be problematic. I've been watching all sorts of group promotions happen lately, often simply groups of authors who get together to offer an attractive giveaway. Many of these types of activities involve grabbing emails for mailing lists. Obviously, there is a right and wrong way to do this. Just because people enter an email to enter a Rafflecopter giveaway (as an example) doesn't give permission to scoop all those email addresses, unless, of course, that was part of the giveaway and people are clear as to what they are doing. Even so, make sure that all these people get a welcome email and the chance to unsubscribe in case they are somewhere they don't want to be.

Quote from MailChimp:

> "Did everyone on your list specifically give you permission to email them? If not, and you've added them to your list because you assume they want to hear from you then you are sending spam"

One last thought before we move to the next book in this collection; encourage interaction with and among your readers. One of the most powerful things you can do is to put a Call to Action statement at the bottom of your newsletter and encourage the sharing of your newsletter. Just like blog posts, many people get to the end of a newsletter and then without a Call to Action, they wander away to look at the next email. Clicking on a share button takes seconds, something that people are happy to do, yet so powerful for you.

BOOK 3 - NEWSLETTERS THAT ROCK

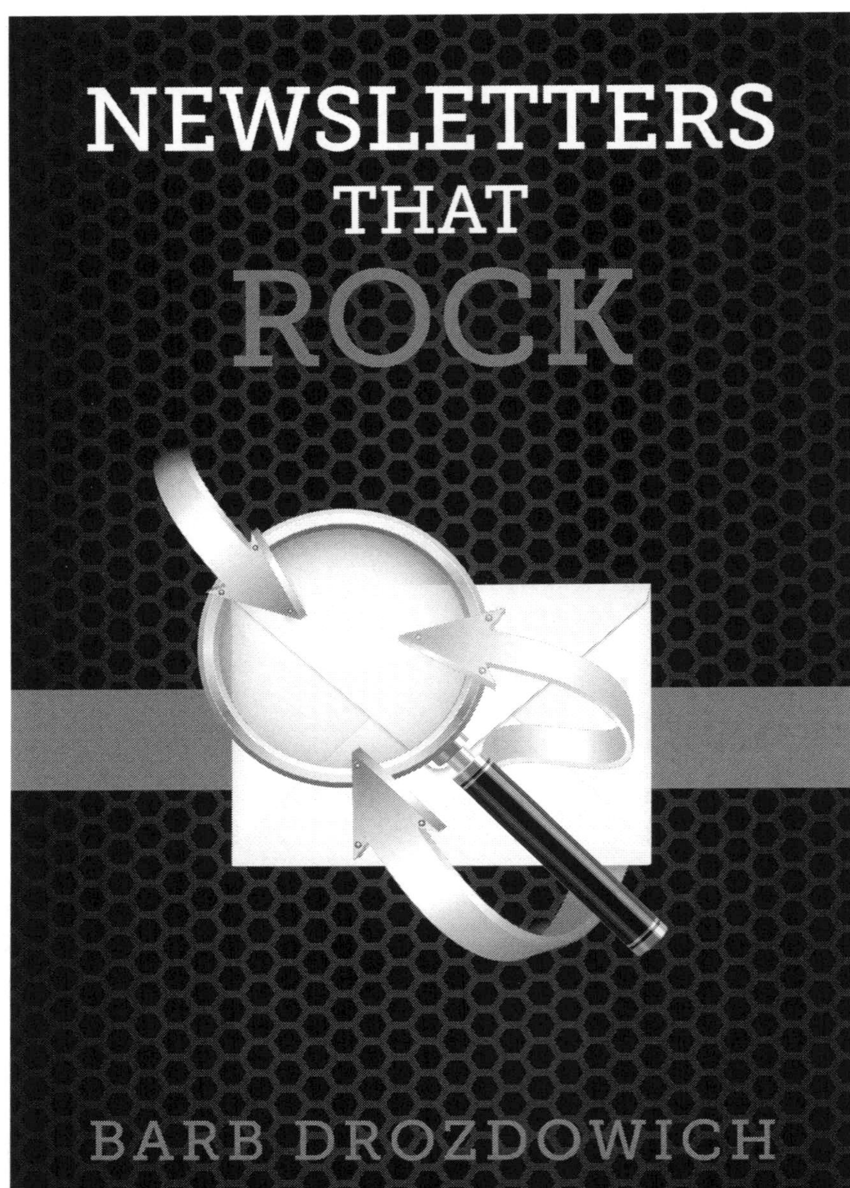
NEWSLETTERS
THAT
ROCK
BARB DROZDOWICH

INTRODUCTION

"Recent articles estimate the average consumer sends and receives 88 emails a day. Now that's a lot of emails to sift through. So how do you make your newsletter stand out from the crowd? What will make your recipients stop in their tracks when they see your latest newsletter sitting in their inbox?" Adestra staff writer

"Commonly thought of as one of the best solutions to generate more sales leads, nurture relationships with existing customers, cross sell and amplify content, email newsletters can be a great source of joy... or stress. They are a great asset when they generate results and deliver satisfying open and click through rates but they can be a real disappointment when they go unopened, or even worse - when the receiver unsubscribes altogether." In Touch CRM

Welcome to the last book of this collection. In this book we're going to talk about what makes a good newsletter. Many people like to say that the creation of a great email is a science not an art. I disagree with that statement. Every audience is different in terms of geographical makeup, composition of ages and genders, genre of books read and that barely touches the surface of potential differences. For an expert to say that there is a one-size-fits-all for newsletters I feel is disingenuous.

Do I feel that there are some commonalities - some best practices? Yes. There is also some science that we can fall back on that will help you understand some of the best practices.

First of all in this book, we're going to talk about the science of reading electronic sources. We're going to follow that with some basic understanding of newsletter layout. We're going to follow this with a chapter on creating the optimal subject line. After that I'm going to share thoughts on best practices from a variety of industries. My intent with this section is to give you lots of different things to think about and lots of ideas to try.

I'll throw some numbers (pulled from a variety of sources) at you to help you understand why I think that this information is important…

21% of recipients report email as Spam even when they know it isn't.
43% of recipients click the Spam button based on the email 'From' name or email address alone.
69% of recipients report an email as Spam based solely on the subject line.
35% of recipients open an email based on the subject line alone.

Do these numbers help you understand why I think this information is important?

Let's get started…

1

THE SCIENCE OF READING ON ELECTRONIC SOURCES

You're probably wondering why I would want to talk about reading on electronic sources. You're probably saying to yourself ...is this really a thing? The answer is yes!

In fact there are a lot of studies that have been performed on how people read on electronic devices or how people differ in the way they read on electronic sources versus paper sources.

Whether you have a smart phone or an E-reader or a tablet or a computer, if you read on any of these you are reading on an electronic source. It doesn't matter whether it's a book, a blog post, an email or official research, if it is on a screen we can make certain assumptions.

Before we start with this I want you to put a picture in your mind. Think about the last time you were around young people - teenagers or early 20s. Did you watch them interacting on their phone? Although I'm going to make some generalizations about this age group, their behavior will apply to most people trying to find information on a phone. The person stands with the phone in one hand and with the other hand uses one finger to scroll. The scrolling may be quick, or it may be slow, but it's unusual to see a person holding a phone and just reading; not getting ready to move the screen. Let's face it, those little screens are pretty small. I read fairly quickly and anytime I'm trying to read something on my phone my finger is moving the screen as I read.

A saying that I came across several years ago about readers having the attention span of a gnat is one that I'm fond of. It seems to encapsulate the scanning behavior that is seen on electronic sources.

Studies on how somebody reads on electronic sources have been going on for decades. Back when I was teaching college, the publishers were starting to talk about offering textbooks electronically, rather than a paper version. Sure, back then (late 80s to early 90s) the technology that we had in terms of e-readers was different. We had computers, but not the level of tablets and smart phones that exist today.

I remember this topic being brought up at a staff meeting by some of my fellow profs. You see, I taught science, and my first response was it would be great not to have to lug around all those big textbooks. At the time the subject went nowhere because the Dean (in my department) didn't feel that publishers would be changing anytime soon. Seems that he was right. Although we did have an information session from a publisher there was still not a lot of movement for several years.

There was a study published in 1997 by a person named Levy. A quote from that study says:

> "The development of digital libraries is participating in a general societal trend toward shallower, more fragmented, less concentrated reading."

In fact there was a study 11 years later that demonstrates this very clearly. In this study people agreed to read a certain piece of text and it was read on a computer screen. The study tracked the movement of the eyeballs to determine not only how much was read, but in what fashion the text was read.

What's really interesting about this study is that the people who took part agreed to read a certain amount of text and then lied about it. Lying might be a strong term. The people honestly felt that they had fulfilled their instructions but the eye tracking results indicated that only 20% of the text was read. When they studied the eye tracking movements, they discovered that generally reading is not a smooth process moving from left to right across the screen. Typically eyes wander over the text, stopping briefly before moving forward or going backwards over text that has been read. Readers tend to fixate or stop on longer words or ones of a different format and they tend to skip over short words. Secondly the beginning of any text is read more thoroughly than the end. This behavior carries forward to websites. I'm sure you've heard that you need to put your most important information above the fold or at the top half of the screen.

So what are the takeaways from this and other studies?

1) Users scan and skim electronic content. The way to deal with this scanning and skimming is to use things like bolded headlines and subheads. If you can include a keyword in a heading or subheading, the person reading will pick up on that word. In addition, you can use devices like bulleted lists to catch attention. The use of pictures is also encouraged.

2) Use plain language - People who are reading electronic sources want to get to the bottom of what they're reading. As we'll talk about in a bit, if somebody is actually invested in what they're reading they will pay a lot more attention. Things like flowery language and excessive descriptions don't really work well in electronic text.

3) Images -There are different kinds of images that you can use in newsletters. Images that convey a message or state information tend to be paid attention to more than decorative pictures. To apply this directly to newsletters, an image that conveys information about an upcoming book signing would be paid attention to more than the text describing the book signing. As we'll discuss further, decorative pictures can also be used as section breaks, or places the reader can rest their eyes.

4) Standard features - Studies show that people who read from electronic sources respond better to norms than differences. If we use the example of a website, people are going to anticipate a header at the top, a section of content, perhaps containing a blog post, and a sidebar off to one side. Sites that depart from this norm create a sense of frustration especially when viewed on a really small screen. If we take this information and apply it to a newsletter, readers are going to anticipate a header graphic at the top of the newsletter. Underneath that some sort of a welcome message and then the information that they're seeking, typically in blocks. We'll talk more about these blocks in the next chapter.

As I mentioned there's been several studies over the years looking at how people read on electronic sources. One of the most interesting things that has been found is that the more a person reads on an electronic device or source, the more automatic the scanning behavior is. So if you compare the reading behavior of a 70 or 80-year-old with the reading behavior of a teenager, the teenager will predominantly read in a scanning behavior, whereas the older person will spend less time reading in this fashion.

The take away from this is to consider your audience. If you are writing a newsletter aimed at younger people, you can guarantee they're going to scan. However if you're aiming your newsletter at an older audience their reading behavior will be somewhat different.

But one point to keep in mind before we move on, is the vast majority of people nowadays view their email on phones. The percentages will differ for different age groups and different geographic regions, but as high as 80% of all email is read on phones. Optimizing electronic sources of reading for viewing on mobile devices is so important that in the last year Google has stepped in with a number of rules. Included are what pop-ups can look like and ensuring that websites are mobile responsive in order to rank on a Google search. Google is concerned with mobile behavior and so should you be.

2

BASIC STRUCTURE OF A NEWSLETTER

In this chapter we're going to talk about the basic structure of the newsletter. As we mentioned in the previous chapter, in terms of reading things on electronic sources, people are drawn to normal. What might be appreciated in real life as one might see in abstract art, or let's say in a paperback book that has an atypical text layout, generally isn't tolerated when it's part of a newsletter or website. Most of the studies that have been done have been in reference to website structure, but parallels can be made to newsletters, as it's a similar structure and similar medium.

People will actually express anger or frustration when confronted with a non-traditional layout.

Although we have touched on this in previous chapters and previous books, let's consolidate all of that information into this chapter. We're going to talk about the basic structure, as well as a few tips and tricks at the end.

At the very top of any newsletter is going to be a header. The header can be a graphic or it can be text. One of the main reasons for an identifiable header at the top of the newsletter is for branding purposes. If your readers are anything like me, they read a lot of books by a lot of different authors. Although you're familiar with your books, readers might need a reminder of who you are and what you write.

Using the same header graphic as you use on your website, or at least the same colors and patterns, will bring a sense of familiarity to your newsletter and will help your readers quickly figure out who this newsletter is from.

Although some experts will recommend regularly changing the graphic at the top of your newsletter, I don't agree with that idea. It is the first thing your readers see once the newsletter opens and it needs to bring a sense of familiarity.

The next section below the header, should be some sort of a greeting. When we talked about deliverability, I mentioned that emails are more likely to be delivered if they're addressed to a person. Just like in the normal email where you address the person that email is going to, you should apply the same principles to a newsletter. In fact many experts suggest that you go one step further and have a welcome statement as the first thing that people read. The welcome statement can be just that - a welcome or an introduction. It can also serve as a type of executive summary also. In other words it can be a short blurb of "In this newsletter we're going to talk about this, this and this." This gives people an idea of what the newsletter is going to contain, and perhaps get them excited about what they're going to read.

Most of the rest of the newsletter is what is considered to be the body. This is where your basic information is contained. As we talked about when describing how to create a newsletter in Mailerlite in book #2 of this collection, the best way to present this information is in blocks that are relatively short, containing keywords, titles and a picture to decorate.

The bottom of any newsletter is called the footer. The footer serves as the ending of a newsletter, but it is also the area that has some standard information as required by law. Things like the unsubscribe link, the mailing address, and perhaps a few other tidbits are typically found in the footer of the newsletter.

. . .

Let's finish off this chapter by talking about a few of the tips and tricks.

1) Newsletter width - This newsletter is going out by email - Some people may view the email in their browser or have an email account like Gmail that is typically viewed in a browser. This doesn't mean that the newsletter should be the typical width of a webpage, however. Often what newsletter programs will do if the newsletter is too wide is cut off the right hand side. No amount of scrolling will make it visible. So typically it is suggested that a newsletter be no more than 600 pixels wide. I typically create them in the range of 550 to 600 pixels.

2) Background Images - Although background images are typically treated differently from graphics within the body of the newsletter, there are fewer and fewer email programs that actually support this functionality. If a background image is something that you insist on as part of the design, make sure the newsletter has a background color as well in case the background image isn't displayed.

3) Fonts - Fonts are a very personal thing, in my experience. Not only do people have strong feelings about serif versus sans-serif fonts, in my experience people like to use unique fonts as part of newsletters. Using unique fonts can be gotten away with to a certain extent with webpages as the website will include, as part of the coding, the fonts. This isn't true of emails. If you want your newsletter to look the same across a wide variety of email programs, stick to the classic fonts like Arial, Helvetica, Tahoma and Times.

4) Balance text to images - Experts like to comment on what the definition of a good balance really is. The reality is no one knows because all email spam filters are different. What we can talk about is best practices. On one end of the spectrum, you don't want a newsletter that has nothing but text. It will be seen as boring and overwhelming to read. On the other end of the spectrum you don't want everything on one graphic with no external text. What is often quoted as the minimum is 2 to 5 lines of text for every image. And as a last reminder, a large number of email programs do not automatically load pictures with the rest of the email, so make sure every picture has an alt text label to let readers know what they're missing and perhaps encourage them to load the pictures

5) Mobile responsive layout - As we've mentioned several times a large percentage of emails are read on a mobile device - via phone or a tablet. Since we can assume that the majority of our newsletters will be read on one of these devices we want to make sure that they are easy to read. In fact, one of the reasons for using an email marketing service is so that you can create a newsletter that will reorganize and present itself properly regardless of what size of screen it is being viewed on. The last thing that you want is a newsletter that shrinks to fit the screen as that would make it difficult to read.

Now that we have finished talking about the basic structure of the newsletter we're going to attack the topic of a subject line.

3

THE SCIENCE OF CREATING GREAT SUBJECT LINES

In this chapter we'll talk about subject lines and the theories on what makes a great one. We're going to talk about some best practices and yes we're probably going to mention spam words.

Before we talk about some of the major theories surrounding the topic of a subject line, let's consider some basic facts. It doesn't take long in a Google search to find out how often people delete an email based on the subject line. I've found numbers as high as 70%. Just like people judge a book by the cover, people will judge a newsletter by its subject line.

I want you to take a few minutes and go to your own email program and look at how email appears. How much room is taken up by whom the email is from, and how much room is taken up by the subject? Do you have an email program that shows you the first 50 or 100 characters of the content of the email? Although it's fine, well and good to say that people will delete an email based on the subject line not all of us actually pay much attention to subject lines when we create the newsletter.

Looking at your own email program, what do you see? Do you see the email address indicating whom the email is from or just the name of the person? Can you easily see subject lines or are they commonly truncated? Can you see the first bit of an email as part of a preview pane? You may have noticed that we talked about the subject line as part of our instruction of Mailerlite in book #2 of this collection, that subject line will allow 150 characters. Again experts will tell you the shorter, the better; others say longer is better and some will say somewhere in the middle is better.

The reality is you want to create a subject line that is typically not truncated by the email program. You want your readers to be able to read the whole line, and keep in mind that a large number of readers view their emails on a mobile device and most of those only show 25 - 30 characters. In order to ensure that your carefully crafted subject line is viewed, don't use all hundred plus characters. In fact I would aim for a top end of about 50 or 55 characters with the subject line front loaded or the hook at the beginning.

The other thing that I'll reiterate at this point is that you want to make sure that your newsletter is from an identifiable person. What that means is you don't want to have just your name in the "from line." Perhaps try your name followed by the title of the book that first interested the person in your list, or the title of your bestseller. That will help recipients of your email remember who you are.

Now that we've talked about the structural issues, let's talk about some of the significant theories surrounding crafting subject lines. As I'm sure you're aware, there is no shortage of blog posts on this subject.

A man named Alex Williams, created the C.U.R.V.E formula for writing email subject lines. Each letter of the word "Curve" stands for an aspect of his theory - Curiosity, Urgency, Relevancy, Value and Emotion. Alex has spent years creating and testing email subject lines. He feels that every good subject line has at least two of these five elements.

Let's talk about each of the elements.

1) Curiosity - How do you make people curious about what you want to share? One of the obvious ways is to ask a question that they would like to know the answer to. This suggestion is to ask open questions not yes or no questions. As you ask these questions you want to make sure that you don't mislead or trick people into thinking there is content in your newsletter that is not there as that will damage trust. One of the examples Alex offers is: "What does reading books have to do with being successful?"

2) Urgency - This part of the formula explains why your reader needs to open your email right now. Inferring that delaying may result in missing out on an amazing offer. This can be a time-sensitive discount, a live event such as a webinar or a training program that has a limited number of spots. Alex suggests that asking for immediate action gets better results than urgent action. Keep in mind that the urgency only works when it's for something that the readers want.

3) Relevancy - The content you send your readers must be relevant to their interests. Kind of a no-brainer, however difficult to do. One of the things that very few people that send out newsletters do, is gather data about their subscribers - ask questions.

4) Value - Typically your subscribers follow you in the first place because they feel that you have something of value to offer. This could be information or books/products. In order to continue providing value to your subscribers you should ask very little in return. That doesn't mean giving away everything for free, but be generous in your offers.

5) Emotion - The decisions that people make are based more on emotions than logic. There is a fair amount of information to support this. Alex feels the best way to trigger an emotion is with sensory language. To clarify, sensory language means sight, sound, touch, taste and smell.

Some examples:

- You haven't seen anything like this before.
- How many times have you heard these three words?
- Why do we feel so bad after a breakup?
- Nothing tastes better than a fresh pizza.
- Does your bathroom smell bad? Here's what to do.

Another prominent theory suggests that all subject lines should have the formula of "Get + Action." In other words what the readers will get and what action do you want them to take. The example that is given "Download the prequel to the best series ever; here's your free copy." There is quite a bit of support for this theory, I think, mainly because it's easy. It's a one-size-fits-all for subject lines. You can state what the person is going to get and combine that with what action you want them to take. Although this theory is clear and simple, I think it's a bit misleading to assume that all subject lines can be crafted in this pattern.

Along the same lines as that theory, many articles will suggest that a good email subject line is designed to get your ideal reader's attention. The only question is how you actually do that. What is suggested is using the formula of: Interest = benefit + curiosity.

In other words I should be able to read your email subject line and feel like I'm going to get something. Hopefully, I'll also read it and wonder what the rest of the email is going to say. If you create a subject line around some sort of a benefit, readers will wonder what could be inside the newsletter.

In fact, there was a famous study at Carnegie Mellon University by a neuroscientist named Lowenstein. He found that when we encounter things that peak our interest but don't reveal "the goods" we have a strong desire to delve further so that we avoid the dissatisfaction of not knowing the outcome. Perhaps this is why an excerpt of an upcoming book in a newsletter has such a positive effect.

Although we want to peak somebody's interest, make them curious, and create a sense of urgency, as was found in the famous psychology study, people are intimidated by too many choices. In fact quite a few experts will suggest that there should only be one goal of the subject line. When people try to cram too much, no choice is made at all.

The study that talks about this was carried out by a psychology professor, Sheena Iyengar. The book on this study is called "The Art of Choosing." Sheena studied people buying jam at a supermarket. She found that more jam was sold on a day when only six different types were offered than on a day when 24 types were offered.

This type of study can translate to a newsletter. When readers are presented with too many choices one would assume they would struggle over which choice to make and therefore not make any or not make enough.

One more famous study from 1987 suggests that finding as little as $.10 was enough to change somebody's mood for the better. That's the basis behind offering free things in a newsletter. You can make somebody's day by offering something free. By association, the suggestion that the newsletter which contains something free is a stimulus to open it.

One last little tidbit to this is that whereas subject lines that peak curiosity and generate a sense of urgency don't tend to work if they are mysterious. It seems that people like to be curious but they are frustrated by ambiguity.

The last theory we'll talk about in this section can be found in the article by Sumo, *The Jade Scroll of the Best Email Subject Lines*. The link to the article is: https://sumo.com/stories/best-email-subject-lines Sumo is a company that has various products to help funnel traffic to websites. They are invested to a certain extent in helping people network with an audience. The Jade Scroll article is simply a list of subject line formulas with an example.

What I liked about the theory found in this article is the wide variety of formulas to choose from. As I'm sure you're gathering, the majority of experts on the topic of subject lines feel that there is a pattern or a formula that good subject lines follow. They certainly feel that patterns and combinations of words give us a starting point to then work from.

In the article mentioned above there were one hundred of the best subject line formulas. Many don't apply to author newsletters - they are more applicable to businesses selling services. However, I've included a number of examples below to get you thinking.

The last call email
The formula is: An event closes in number of hours
The example is: Book sale ends tomorrow

The urgency email
The formula is: The action needs to be taken right now

The example is: Open this email right now

The list email
The formula is: The (number) ways to (benefit)
The example is: My top favorite books from last year

The welcome email
The formula is: Welcome to (Person's Reader Group)
The example is: Welcome to Barb's Street Team

The how to email
The formula is: How to (achieve desired results)
The example is: How to Manage your Images in a WordPress Blog

The branded newsletter email
The formula is: (name of newsletter)(issue number)
The example is: Barb's Newsletter #34

The new post email
The formula is: (new post) (content or title)
The example is: New Post How to embed Amazon Affiliate links

The what if email
The formula is: What if (negative result)
The example is: What if Facebook closed their doors tomorrow?

The versus email
The formula is: (subject) vs (subject)
The example is: The Good Girls of Romance vs The Bad Girls of Romance

The authority email

The formula is: (authority's name) (topic plus secret or tips)
The example is: Mark Dawson's secret tips to succeeding with Facebook Ads

The flash sale email
The formula is: (flash sale)(name of product)(discount)
The example is: Flash Sale: The Author's Presence 50% today only

The what I learned email
The formula is: What I learned after (accomplishment)
The example is: What I learned after surveying 700+ book bloggers

The quick announcement email
The formula is: A quick announcement: (topic)
The example is: Quick announcement: My next book is live on Amazon!

The call out email
The formula is: (audience) (topic)
The example: Readers get your next sizzling read here

The social proof email
The formula is: proof that (works)
The example is: Over 500 reviews on Amazon say that The Author's Presence is very helpful.

The question email
The formula is: (question)
The example is: Am I the only one looking for a new book to read?

The You email
The formula is: You, a (desired result)

The example is: You, a best-selling author?

The imagine email
The formula is: Imagine (desired result)
The example is: Imagine a Kindle full of books.

The seasonal discount email
The formula is: Save (discounts) on (items) this (season)
The example is: Save 50% and fill your Kindle this winter

The truth about email
The formula is: The truth about (topic/ person)
The example is: The truth about Kindle Unlimited

The best of email
The formula is: The best of (item)
The example is: The best of Kindle Worlds books

The can't be wrong email
The formula is: (number) people can't be wrong
The example is: 500 Amazon reviewers can't be wrong

That's quite a selection of formulas. I've included quite a few examples, and I'm sure that you can come up with other examples of your own.

The last subject that I'll be mentioning in this section is the wide variety of tools available to help with the creation of a perfect subject line. One of my favorites is by Coschedule. They have what they call a Headline Analyzer and it can be found at:

http://coschedule.com/headline-analyzer.

This free tool will analyze each word as well as the combination of words that you type in and present a score. Although it is designed to create eye-catching headlines for blog posts, I find it helpful when creating subject lines for newsletters as well. In fact, a simple Google search will let you know that there are lots of paid services that you can buy to help with subject line generation.

As I'm sure you've realized, I'm of the mind that there isn't a one size fits all solution to the problem of creating the perfect subject line. What is attractive to a YA audience would not be to horror aficionados. I encourage you to play with some of the ideas in this chapter and see how your audience responds.

4

THE SCIENCE OF CREATING EMAILS THAT ARE EAGERLY ANTICIPATED

Like the previous chapter on creating the perfect subject line, all you have to do is type 'Eagerly Anticipated Emails' into a Google search and you get hundreds of suggestions. The common theme running through this book is that all audiences are not identical and what works for a marketing email may not work when communicating with readers. That is of course why I try to separate Marketing advice from other communication advice.

When talking about the science of creating emails that are eagerly anticipated, one of the best sources is Pat Flynn. Pat is an entrepreneur with great websites, an outstanding podcast, and several books under his belt. He tends to have down-to-earth, practical advice. On the subject of emails that are wanted by your readers, he talks about FOMO, or the Fear Of Missing Out. He says that all people have this fear.

A quote from his article, How to Train Your Subscribers to Open Your Emails Every Time you Send:

> "When you create a gap between what people know, and what people want to know, they feel compelled to fill that gap."

Although the "Fear Of Missing Out" is often taken advantage of when creating the subject lines, this can also be leveraged when trying to create eagerly anticipated newsletters. He actually says that:

> "...when your subscribers expect great things from your emails, they will open every single email and will always look forward to the next."

He goes on to say that upfront massive value is really important. In fact, if you want people to open your emails, reward them with small victories. These small victories don't always have to be a free book, but they should be something that is of great value to your audience.

A common thread through most of the advice about newsletters is to treat each of your subscribers as friends. The comments about informal friendly tone go towards an overall feeling that people get from your newsletter.

In an article in Medium:

https://medium.com/@postmasternow/guidelines-for-creating-eagerly-anticipated-emails-dbe4bf694725#.ofk4rn76f)

creators of newsletters are encouraged to shift their thinking.

> "It's not a list. They are not 'subscribers.'"

You are encouraged to see your list as a group of friends, not just a list of email addresses. You are encouraged to **not** see subscribers but to see people. The gist of this article is if you change the way you think that will come through in your content and your approach. Although I've cited one article, the idea of your tone changing when you view your audience as friends is not a new one or uncommon one. Many of the blogging experts offer the same advice. The friendly tone, informal language, relatability ideas are very common in the literature.

If we move forward with the idea of emails that are eagerly anticipated and have great value, let's talk about how we can provide great value to our readers without just providing free books.

You should know your audience or you should work to get to know your audience. Other than a free book what else would they value? Put yourself in their shoes. I have one newsletter that I get every month that tells me of all of the author-related events in my general area. I actually go to very few events, but I appreciate this newsletter because it lets me know of the possibilities. If I choose not to go, that's my choice, but at least I know about the events.

Another example, from several authors that I work with, is the sharing of recipes. Generally speaking the recipes are accompanied with mouthwatering pictures. I'm not much of a cook, but just the sight of these treats is enough to make me want to try.

One last example that I've seen work very well is suggesting a book that you've read and why you loved it. As authors we're all readers. Why not share something that you enjoy with your audience without any expectation of making money from it?

Other ideas to throw out there to get you thinking:

1. Consider creating a "list" email - maybe it's a list of the reading order of your latest series. Maybe it has nothing to do with your writing whatsoever but it's valuable to your audience and it's an email they'll want to keep
2. Consider creating an "insider's" email - behind-the-scenes information on books that you've written for your readers. Perhaps share some deleted scenes.
3. Consider creating a "how to" list. This is likely a better fit for a nonfiction author, but think about your content and see if that lends itself towards creating a series of how-to's
4. Consider creating "the best of" list. Readers react really well to things like best books for the previous year, and if you blog perhaps a list of your most popular blog posts. I find that on my blog there are certain posts that just regularly get traffic. Obviously they rank well and people find them helpful. I like to mention them in a newsletter periodically so that my readers will have a point of reference. Two posts that come to mind, one on putting Amazon affiliate links in place and the other one on the

proper size of images on all of the various social media platforms. Both seem to be solid sources of information for readers.

One final thought on creating eagerly anticipated emails, is with respect to timing. Regularity is better than irregularity when it comes to communicating with your readers. Many authors will send out a newsletter once a month at the first of the month or the middle of the month and readers get used to that schedule. Because of this, if something happens in terms of deliverability your readers will miss the email and perhaps go looking for it. The other thing that regular communication does is help you keep your list current. As we've mentioned in previous sections of this collection, a mailing list is considered to be stale if it's more than six months old and people are said to change email addresses frequently. Reminding your readers that they can either submit their new email address to you or use the 'update preferences' link (if available from your service) helps keep your list fresh and up-to-date.

Lastly, think about what time of day or what day of the week you want to send a newsletter. Marketing types will tell you to send an email in the wee hours on either a Monday or Tuesday morning so that it is sitting waiting to be read when your readers get to work. The vast majority of emails that I help to send are not work related (for the receivers). Even if they give out a work email address, they may not feel comfortable reading your newsletter during work time. Typically the advice for 'hobby newsletters" is to send them out on a weekend. People generally have more leisure time on the weekends and can give your newsletter better attention. Many Email Marketing Services have the ability to let you schedule your newsletter in advance and will also allow you to send it out at a specific time for various time zones. This is handy for your international readers. Ultimately, let your stats help you understand the best time to send out a newsletter. Try various times and see what the response is!

5

TIPS AND HINTS TO MAKE A GREAT NEWSLETTER

In this final chapter I want to pull together information from a wide variety of sources. I've said throughout this book, I don't actually believe there is a right way and a wrong way to communicate with your readers. As we've discussed, there are certainly best practices, but the experts out there that infer that their way is the only way, I think are being shortsighted.

As I've pointed out before, different audiences have different compositions. If you are an author who writes women's fiction, I wouldn't anticipate your audience to be primarily male. Likewise if you write YA fiction, I wouldn't anticipate your audience to be mostly made up of seniors. Let's face it, you want to communicate in an appropriate manner in order to connect with your audience. So other than the technical details that we've talked about in previous chapters and books of this collection, now I want to pull together pieces of advice from a wide variety of sources. Some will be appropriate for your audience, some won't. The idea here though is to give you lots of things to think about and lots of different ideas to try.

One of the first things that I suggest to my authors is to sit down with a cup of coffee, tea, perhaps a mug of beer and a piece of paper or a laptop. Write or type a list of ideas. Think about how you want to be communicated to as a reader because although you're an author you are also a reader. Almost every newsletter expert out there, regardless of the audience that they talk about, suggests being upfront and clear with your audience. Let them know in advance what your intent is so they can make an informed choice. Try to make a big picture plan of what you want to do with your newsletters. Not that this needs to be written in stone, but it will give you a starting point, and it will also give you something to tell potential subscribers.

Now let's go through my list of tips and hints from a variety of experts and see if any of them resonate with you.

1) Informal, friendly tone

Many experts offer some version of a comment on the tone of the newsletter. They'll say to use an informal, friendly tone. The article that I like the best was the one that advises viewing people who sign up to the newsletter as friends not subscribers and not numbers. I honestly feel that if you see the people on your newsletter as potential friends it will automatically change your approach and your tone. At the same time you don't want to be overly familiar and possibly offend people, but I feel that you can be friendly and informal without causing offense.

2) Put together a nice mix of images and text

One of the first questions I received during a seminar that I presented on this subject was with regards to the proportion of text and images. The person wanted to know what the perfect proportion is. I don't think that there is a perfect proportion. I feel that, as with many online sources, we need to inform and entertain at the same time. In order to do that we use pictures to educate, we use pictures as a bit of a mental break, and as a dividing line of sorts. As for what is right for your audience, I encourage you to try a variety of different things, but try to stay in the middle somewhere. In other words don't create a newsletter that is all text; don't create a newsletter that is all pictures, create something that is in the middle and then pay attention to your analytics.

3) Clever call to action buttons

Many experts suggest having call to action buttons. Depending on how buttons are created they frequently are an image. Since we know that so many people's email programs don't open images automatically, I question the logic of this advice. To be clear I'm questioning the advice of having a button I'm not questioning the advice of having a clever call to action. A call to action is often what's missing from many newsletters. Whether you do this using a button or simply text, make sure that you have a call to action, at least one.

4) Use "you" not "I" - don't talk about yourself

Some of the more standard advice for newsletters is to use the newsletter to keep your readers up to date on what you are doing and the progress of your projects. There is a minority of the experts that advise not talking about yourself. And what they suggest is simply taking information that you were going to share about yourself and turning it around and presenting it in a different way. As an example, instead of saying "I have a new book to be released next month," say something like: "You will have a new book in your hot little hands by this time next month." Play with this idea and see how you can remove the "I" from your newsletters.

5) Consider putting an executive summary at the beginning

The idea of an executive summary comes out of the experts from the marketing camp. An executive summary can be thought of as a preview to the content you are going to cover in the newsletter. Several of the marketing newsletters that I subscribe to literally have an executive summary at the beginning and in some cases a table of contents. Generally speaking these newsletters are fairly long. I don't suggest something of that length for authors; however, having a brief preview at the beginning certainly can't hurt. Keep in mind that a large percentage of your audience will be viewing your email using an email program that has a preview pane. A bit of a teaser at the beginning will keep people reading to the end.

6) Consider a picture of yourself and a custom signature at the bottom

Many professionals and other marketing experts suggest including a picture of yourself as well as a signature at the bottom of the newsletter. For most authors I don't think that the picture is all that necessary, but it is a fairly commonly known fact that people react more positively when they see you as a real person. So, consider including a picture of yourself as part of the full package of communication with readers. As for the second part, a custom signature, I feel that this is missing from many newsletters. When we're talking about a custom signature I don't literally mean a graphical representation of your name in a fancy font. I mean a friendly and informative sign off or ending to your newsletter. Keep in mind that many people will get to the end of a newsletter and wander away. You want to leave them with an uplifting thought or give them some pieces of information, or perhaps give them some instruction. Newsletters that are shared amongst friends are more powerful than those that are kept to the readers. You would be amazed at the number of people that will share your newsletter with their friends if you ask them to. Consider putting together a couple of sentences of thanks and instruction for the bottom of your next newsletter and see what your readers do.

7) Use headers & sub- headers

If we go back to the information that I shared about people reading on electronic sources, you'll remember that the reading behavior is more of a scanning behavior. Although above we've talked about including pictures as a piece of information, as a section break, or simply as a rest for the eyes, you can use a series of headers and sub-headers as attention-getters and division points as well. A keyword containing header or a sub header that is informative and that stands out from the rest of the text will be caught by the eyes of someone who's scanning. This is something they would typically stop and read before moving on. As you put together your next newsletter hopefully following some of the suggestions that you learned in this book, consider including attention-getting headers at various points in your newsletter to share important information.

8) Make sure important content is bolded

The advice of making sure that important parts are bolded is something that is overlooked. Most fiction authors are trained to write in normal font or perhaps the odd italic section. It's fairly uncommon to find words bolded in a novel. So making sure that important points stand out from the rest of the text in a newsletter is an unfamiliar action for most authors. For examples of what to bold, I would suggest dates and locations of events, and buy links for books, to name a few.

9) Use blocks of color

Many people suggest using the odd block of color in your newsletter. You'll notice I said the odd block of color! A newsletter that has one block of color that stands out is more effective than a newsletter that has a different color for each section. A multicolored newsletter can be difficult to read. If you have an important piece of information that you want to share, I suggest you put it in a colored section either really close to the beginning of your newsletter or in the middle so that it stands out from its surroundings.

. . .

10) Use a text call to action that doesn't say "read more" but belongs in the content

This piece of advice is similar to the comment about call to action buttons above, but it goes more to talking about the relevancy of links. Remember a spammer's trick is to have a clickable link that says "click here," or some other phrase that is not helpful. What is generally suggested is that you embed a hyperlink in the text of a descriptive sentence. Instead of saying "buy now" you could say "my book is available for purchase now and can be found on Amazon, Barnes & Noble, Kobo, and iTunes," with each of the retailers having a clickable link to the buy page. Readers will understand if they want to buy a copy they click on the appropriate link.

11) Keep it focused

Don't use a newsletter as a vehicle for an unrelated content dump. A really important piece of advice is to keep your newsletter focused. Although at times chatty, newsy newsletters are fun to create and fun to read, but keep in mind how valuable people's time is. Also keep in mind your audience. The majority of people will appreciate a helpful informative newsletter, but wouldn't necessarily appreciate one that rambles on and on and on.

12) Give it some personality

What I think is a really important piece of advice is to give your newsletter some personality that reflects the perception that subscribers to your mailing lists are your friends. One of the reasons that author blogs can be so important to readers is because they allow readers a glimpse into an author's world. They allow readers to get to know the author as a person in addition to enjoying their books. The same will be true of a newsletter. Remember that you don't want to ramble on, but you do want to allow your personality to shine through in your newsletter.

. . .

13) Does your newsletter reflect you or your brand?

In an author's busy world of creating books as fast as they can for voracious readers, managing social media, as well as various in-person events, sometimes we forget that our newsletter is more than a vehicle to convey some information. It is part of our brand as an author. An author's brand is often something that is stressed about but in fact it can be very straightforward. Branding will go to colors and an overall look that you carry across your website and all of your various social media, but it will also go to the tone and the subject matter that you convey. Your readers read your books because they like the information that you share and they like the way that you do it. If you write a book that is edgy, peppered with swearwords and dark humor, carry some of that forward into your newsletter. However, if you write sweet romance, a newsletter that is edgy, peppered with swearwords, and dark humor will not necessarily be appreciated.

14) Use a similar header to your website and it will carry forward the brand

The colors and the graphics used in a newsletter have been talked about previously in this book, however it is important to remind you of this again. As above when talking about your brand, we talk about colors and graphical images frequently. You want to make sure that there is a similar look and feel to your newsletter and your website and your other social media accounts. Take pity on the voracious readers that have trouble remembering one author from another. Help them remember who you are and what you write; help them become familiar and recognize your brand.

15) The footer is as important as the header

As important as the header is to a newsletter, the footer is also important. Not only are the contact details necessary to be compliant with legalities, but the footer will also be part of the standard structure. It will help your readers understand that they've gotten to the end of the newsletter. It is not uncommon for email programs to truncate newsletters these days, and the presence of a footer brings a visual end that most people recognize.

16) Make it easy for people to unsubscribe, and don't remove the unsubscribe link from the footer

As we've mentioned previously, you need to make it easy for people to unsubscribe. The last thing you want to do is remove the unsubscribe link from the footer of your newsletter; and yes people do that. You want to allow people to have a graceful out if they no longer want to hear what you want to share. The last thing you want them doing is clicking on that junk or spam button on their email program. Consider putting an unsubscribe text link or button right near the beginning of a newsletter. Not everybody is as technical as others, and making that unsubscribe link easy to find will be appreciated.

17) Build your subscribers expectations

The piece of advice of building your subscribers expectations is an important one. You want to make sure that you give your subscribers or readers what you tell them you're going to give them. If you say you're going to email once a month, then email once a month. At the same time try to make it so that your readers are eagerly anticipating the next newsletter that they get from you.

18) Keep an eye on the analytics

In my experience, I find that authors either completely ignore analytics because they don't know what to do with them, or they misunderstand the meaning of certain pieces of information. I hope with the information that I've given you in book 2 of this collection on the available stats will give you a better idea of what you should be looking at and what you should be paying attention to. And generally speaking if you are emailing an established list there shouldn't be a lot of peaks and valleys in your analytics. An audience that is happy with the newsletters that you're sending generally speaking will continue to be happy. Because of this, a sudden increase or decrease in open rate or click through rate should be investigated.

19) Encourage feedback

You should encourage feedback from your readers in a variety of different ways. Although I understand the pain of having a massively overstuffed inbox, you should be encouraging communication with your readers. Encourage them to respond to the newsletters if they have something that they want to share with you. Encourage them to share your newsletters with their friends to widen your audience.

20) Always be on the lookout for interesting stuff to share; don't make it all about you

As we mentioned in a previous point don't make the newsletter all about you. Most voracious readers are always on the lookout for a new author to read, or a new book to get their hands on. Giving away the Kindle version of a book that you've read and enjoyed or perhaps a book that a fellow author friend has written will win you a lot of brownie points but only cost you a couple of dollars. And as I recently witnessed when one of my authors shared a decadent banana cream dessert recipe, complete with a mouthwatering picture, non-book items are appreciated by many as well.

21) Stay regular. There is a fine line between keeping people updated and spamming

You want to try to be regular in your communication with your mailing list. As I've said above there's a fine line between keeping people updated and spamming. The last thing you want to do is annoy people with excessive newsletters. Watch your analytics and try and find the sweet spot for communicating with your specific group of readers.

22) Give something back - People know when they are being sold to

This point of giving something back is similar to the previous point of talking about another author, another book. People know when they're being sold to, and it's okay to sell to people. But if the only thing that you communicate to your mailing list is information on how to buy your books, people will gradually tune out. Consider giving away somebody else's book to a lucky winner; consider sharing cute pictures or interesting information that has nothing to do with your readers spending money. If you've been at a conference recently, share some pictures and a unique story. Readers will appreciate being treated as friends, not just a wallet.

23) Always test before you send.

Make sure it looks good on desktop and mobile. As the saying goes: test test test. The last thing that you want is to send out an email littered with typos. Try to find somebody who's willing to proofread your newsletter for you, as a second set of eyes she is always more likely to catch mistakes. Although many of the email marketing services have a preview functionality, don't hesitate to send a sample email to yourself. If you have access to a phone and a tablet, view your newsletter on different devices whenever possible.

24) Offer value

The piece of advice of offering value is to a certain extent repetitive of several of the other pieces of advice above, yet somewhat different. Yes, we can share news with our subscribers, share interesting recipes perhaps, and occasionally hope that they buy a book from us, but more importantly, we want to try to add value to their inbox. Try to create a newsletter that adds something, that offers value to your readers. This idea of adding value, I believe, is completely dependent on the audience and the needs of the audience, or perhaps the wants of the audience. Don't hesitate to ask your subscribers questions but only if you're going to pay attention to the answers.

25) Leverage evergreen content

Working with "evergreen" content is something that marketing types and bloggers are really familiar with. Evergreen content is content that is not dependent on time. So, for example, announcing a book release is time-dependent; it only happens once. Sharing a story that could've happened anywhere at any time would be an example of evergreen content. What is evergreen content for you, specifically, is a question that only you can answer. Think about information that you've sent out in previous newsletters and think about other things that you share in other ways. See if you can reuse any of this content. Brush it up, dust it off and maybe add a new graphic and share it again. Evergreen content can continue to give value to your readers long after it was originally created.

26) Personalize the newsletter; address it to a first name

In the deliverability section of this collection we talked about personalizing a newsletter. We talked about how it increases the deliverability because the spam filters will see that you have some information about the person whom you're emailing. Let's face it though, it's friendly to address subscribers by name. It makes them feel like you are talking to them personally.

27) Keep it simple in terms of content.

Don't try to cram too much information in. This piece of information is similar to a previous point of not using a newsletter to serve as an info dump. Just like that survey we talked about of people's activity when they are presented with too many choices of types of jam, if you cover too much information, or have too many choices for people to make, they likely won't make any decisions at all. So keep your information simple straightforward and relevant.

28) Keep it simple in terms of the style

The advice of keeping your newsletter simple in terms of style is a good one on so many different levels. As we talked about in previous sections, using background graphics or complicated looks for a newsletter are not necessarily appreciated by those who read newsletters on mobile devices. Darker colors and odd fonts can be difficult to read, and, in fact, often don't translate properly from email program to email program. Consider sticking with an easy to read standard font, crisp black text and quieter background colors.

29) Make it clear who the newsletter is from

Although there are requirements for being clear about who the newsletter is from, make sure that you are doing a good job of identifying yourself and relating to your audience. The example that is often given is making your newsletter from you, your name, and then stating that you're the author of a certain series or that you're the author of a certain book. This allows your recipients to be very clear about whom the newsletter is from.

30) Use bulleted lists and white space

Use bold text, headers & sub-headers, and attractive images; also consider including features like bulleted lists or numbered lists as part of your information presentation. Whitespace is also important. It allows people's eyes to have a break, and it also prevents your newsletter from looking too crowded.

. . .

31) Share expert advice, testimonials, upcoming events

Many marketing types will suggest that you share expert advice, testimonials, and the like. This doesn't necessarily translate well to the author and book world, unless of course, you write nonfiction. However don't hesitate to share thoughts from other readers about your books. We often call this social proof; it helps other people realize the general consensus of our work. If you're going to be attending a conference or a book signing or a book festival, share the news with your readers. To a large degree we consider our online audience to be a global audience, but you never know who's going to be in the area and available to drop by a live event.

32) Balance your content

Not every one wants to or can spend. It is suggested you have one promo for every three pieces of information. So for every time you want people from your newsletter to buy a book you need to have three other occasions where you simply share information with them and not require them to reach for their wallet. I think this is solid advice.

I've reached the end of my long list of hints. I hope this collection of tips and hints from the world of newsletter design gives you many options to consider.

CONCLUSION

We have reached the end of our journey though all the parts that combine to encompass the topic of communicating with your readers. Lots of ideas to spur your creativity. Lots of solid information to improve your confidence. As I mentioned in various parts of this collection, don't hesitate to use me as a guinea pig for your initial efforts. I'm always happy to share a thought or two.

Until we meet again over the next topic I decide to attack, have fun and enjoy communicating with your readers!

In today's world of book sales, all authors need book reviews from readers posted to the various online retailers. Since you picked up one of my books, I am assuming you are an author - a writer. I encourage you to post an honest review of this book, when you are finished, to the retail site you purchased it from. This action you will help you experience what you will ask your readers to do. It is easier to ask this of your readers if you understand the process.

Thank you so much!

BIBLIOGRAPHY

Adestra staff writer. "What Makes a Great Newsletter?" Jan 17, 2015 http://www.adestra.com/what-makes-a-great-newsletter/

Brodie, Ian. "Email Marketing for Coaches and Consultants." April 20, 2012 https://www.ianbrodie.com/email-marketing-for-coaches-and-consultants/

Campaigner staff writer. "Top 5 tips on writing great email newsletters." http://www.campaigner.com/resource-center/getting-started/top-5-tips-on-writing-great-email-newsletters.aspx

Chaffey Dave. "Digital Marketing Trends for 2017: Essential Digital marketing megatrends that will give you the edge in the new year." Jan 14, 2017 http://www.smartinsights.com/email-marketing/email-commuinications-strategy/statistics-sources-for-email-marketing

Fernandez, Mary. 73 Proven and Simple Ways to Grow Your Email List July 6, 2016 http://optinmonster.com/73-proven-and-simple-ways-to-grow-your-list/

Flynn, Pat. "How to Train Your Subscribers to Open your Emails Every Time You Send." https://www.smartpassiveincome.com/how-to-train-your-subscribers-to-open-your-emails-every-time-you-send/

Furgison, Lisa "25 Comical Subject lines + Tips for Funny Writing." Jan 7, 2017 http://www.verticalresponse.com/blog/25-comical-subject-lines-tips-for-funny-writing/

Lui, Ziming. "Reading behavior in the digital environment." http://www.emeraldinsight.com/doi/abs/10.1108/00220410510632040

Matzner, Ryan. "Why You Should Use Newsletter Services Instead of Sending Mass Emails Yourself." Mar 1, 2016. http://www.bluefountainmedia.com/blog/why-you-should-use-newsletter-services-instead-of-mass-e-mailing-yourself/

Nielson, Jakob. "How Little Do Users Read?" https://www.nngroup.-com/articles/how-little-do-users-read/

Oliphant, Kirsten. "How to Grow Your Email List." Dec 15, 2016. http://janefriedman.com/grow-email-list/

Pitre, Andy. "25 Simple Ways to Grow Your Email List." March 13, 2015 http://blog.hubspot.com/blog/tabid/6307/bid/32028/25-Clever-Ways-To-Grow-Your-Email-Marketing-List/

Sarria, Danavir. "The Jade Scroll of the Best Email Subject Lines." April 12, 2016 https://sumo.com/stories/best-email-subject-lines

Soulo, Tim. "5 Creative Ways to Grow Your Email List." Feb 29, 2016 http://www.socialmediaexaminer.com/5-creative-ways-to-grow-your-email-list/

Virgillito, Dan. "Top Features to Look For In An Email Marketing Software." May 29, 2015 https://www.elegantthemes.com/blog/resources/top-features-to-look-for-in-an-email-marketing-software

Zhel, Martin. "How to Write Catchy E-mail Subject Lines and Increase Open Rates." Jan 18, 2016 https://www.mailmunch.co/blog/how-to-write-catchy-e-mail-subject-lines-and-increase-open-rates/

Zheleva, Didi. "What makes a good email newsletter? 7 key ingredients for a successful email newsletter." Aug 7, 2016 http://www.intouchcrm.com/7-key-ingredients-for-a-successful-email-newsletter/

READER GROUP

Interested in getting some helpful hints and some helpful videos to your inbox? As I'm sure you are aware, authors are encouraged to give away free book to encourage people to join their mailing lists.

My books are different - they solve a problem. Just because you picked up one of my books doesn't mean you want a free book on a completely different topic. Because of this, I offer subscribers to my mailing list, free help - usually in the form of blog posts or YouTube Videos. I let everyone know about new releases and offer money off of my online courses.

If this sounds like something you would be interested in, join me at: http://bakerviewconsulting.com/reader-list/

GLOSSARY

Blog – A blog is a type of website, which allows information to be added in a static fashion as well as a serial fashion. It can be run on a wide variety of platforms or programs.

Blog Feed/Feed – The Blog Feed, typically shortened to "Feed," is also known as RSS or RSS feed. A Blog feed or a RSS feed is a standard Internet technology that allows updates of your blog to be delivered to various places – other websites like Goodreads or into feedreaders like Feedly. In terms of format, it's typically your blog's URL followed by a slash and then the word 'feed' or http://yourdomain.com/feed. It is possible that your blog's feed is different.

Blogging Platform – A Blogging Platform is the program used to operate or run a blog. There are several – the most popular being WordPress, Blogger, and Weebly.

Bounced Email - A bounced email is one that isn't successfully sent for a variety of reasons.

Branding – Branding is the combination of the look, feel, and tone that creates a unified and identifiable collection of information.

Click rates (are also called click through rates) - This number is also expressed as a percentage. Typically this number refers to how many successfully delivered campaigns received at least one click.

Deliverability - Deliverability is getting emails into inboxes.

Domain – also known as a URL – is the address of a website. It's typically in the format of http://yourdomainname.com

Domain Based or paid email addresses - a domain-based email address has the domain of a website as the last part of the address and typically a first name is the first part. The format is firstname@yourdomain.com

Email Firewalls - An email firewall will look at all incoming email as well as outgoing email and collect information about it. Not all firewalls are identical but what is common amongst them is that they monitor the behavior of people sending email and they communicate with one another.

Email Spam Filters - Spam filters are programs that will scan all email to determine whether it should be delivered or not. These filters use a variety of criteria to judge incoming email.

Footer – The footer is the space at the very bottom of your website or blog or newsletter. In some cases it can hold information in addition to a copyright statement.

Header – the Header is the part of a website or newsletter and generally runs from side to side. It can also be used to refer to the top of a blog post – the area where the title is seen.

Hosting company – A Host or Hosting company is a business that has a collection of servers or big computers and sells space on those servers for people to run a blog or website. Examples would be Site Ground, GoDaddy or InMotion Hosting.

Open rates - The open rate is typically expressed as a percentage. This number will tell you how many successfully delivered campaigns are opened by your readers.

Plugin – a piece of code added to a blog to perform a function on that blog. An example of a Plugin is Akismet – it helps segregate spam into a specific folder. Sometimes a Plugin can also function as a **Widget**. In that case, it will have a function on the sidebar of a blog or website. An example of that would be an **Image Widget**.

Post or blog post – A collection of words and pictures that are published and then visible on that blog. The word "Post" is frequently used to refer to an entry (often words and pictures) put on Facebook, Twitter, or other social media.

Search engine – A Search Engine is a very complicated computer program that searches a collection of websites to find entries for given words. An example is Google.

SEO – SEO stands for Search Engine Optimization. SEO is a collection of activities we perform on blogs/websites that make it easier for search engines to find and search them. These activities range from careful use of keywords, to linking to other blogs, to the addition of helpful information to pictures, among other examples.

Sidebar – The area on one or both sides of a website or blog. It contains content that's placed there often in the form of widgets or gadgets.

Sending reputation - The server and domain that your emails are sent from builds up reputation over time with other email services. Because of this, the reputation of the sending server or where emails are sent from is quite important.

Spam - Typically the word spam refers to an unwanted email, an email that arrives in the inbox that wasn't requested. It can also refer to an email that contains content that is unwanted or offensive

URL – The direct link or hyperlink to a post. It can be referred to as a Domain, but can also be used to show the exact link to a specific entry on a website.

User Engagement - it refers to if, and how, your readers engage with your newsletter.

Website – A site on the Internet

Widget – A collection of code used to perform a specific function (usually) on the sidebar of a website or blog. An example of a widget is a Mailerlite widget which will allow a signup form to appear where this widget is placed.

ABOUT THE AUTHOR

Social Media and Wordpress Consultant Barb Drozdowich has taught in colleges, universities and in the banking industry. More recently, she brings her 15+ years of teaching experience and a deep love of books to help authors develop the social media platform needed to succeed in today's fast evolving publishing world. She delights in taking technical subjects and making them understandable by the average person. She owns Bakerview Consulting and manages the popular blog, Sugarbeat's Books, where she talks about Romance novels.

She is the author of 27 books, over 60+ YouTube videos, an online Goodreads course and an online WordPress course, all focused on helping authors and bloggers. Barb lives in the mountains of British Columbia with her family.

Barb can be found on her Book Blog, Business Blog, Pinterest, Goodreads, and Youtube

To Learn More:
barbdrozdowich.com
barb@bakerviewconsulting.com

ALSO BY BARB DROZDOWICH

All my books start with a problem that needs a solution - with a group of authors letting me know about a subject that they don't understand. I take it, break it down and see if I can add some clarity.

The books I've written attack the subjects of:

1) Understanding the world of Book Bloggers, Book Reviewers and book reviews

2) Understanding all the parts and pieces of an author's online presence at a beginner's level

3) Understand the world of book promotions

4) Understanding What to blog, How to blog and Why to blog for authors

5) Understand how to use Goodreads as a tool of networking and communication with readers

6) Understand mailing lists and newsletters

7) Understand how to self-publish a book regardless of what country you live in

8) Understand how to improve your website

During a recent workshop I gave on self-publishing, I walked participants through an exercise to help them understand the power of e-readers as well as the limits of e-readers. I was talking about the fact that not all e-readers can make use of clickable links as not all are connected to the internet or have browser capabilities. We also talked about creating links that readers from a variety of countries can actually use - my example was around solely using an Amazon.com link. Suddenly the light went in my own head about all of the clickable links I put in my books. So…going forward I'm directing everyone to a page that contains information about all of my books and buy links that are associated with those books. The link is easy to type in manually or click on if you have the ability. It is: https://readerlinks.com/mybooks/733

All of my books are also found on my business blog (http://bakerviewconsulting.com) and my author website (http://barbdrozdowich.com).

4 of my books are permanently free.

My books are:

The Author's Guide to Working with Book Bloggers

The Author's On-Line Presence

The Author's Guide to Book Promotion

The Book Blogger Platform

The Author's Guide to Goodreads

Blogging for Authors

The Complete Mailing List Toolkit

Strategies to Grow Your List

Newsletters That Rock

Get Your Emails Delivered

The Author's Guide to Self-Publishing for Canadians

How to Self-Publish a Book

Book Reviews for Author Success

Website Tips & Tricks

How to Optimize Your Social Media

How to Target Book Blogger for Optimize Results

Top Advice for Authors Promoting Their Books

Book Blogger Survey

On-Line Video Courses:

As thanks for reading one of my books, I offer a coupon for 50% off any of my courses. The website that describes all my courses is Author's Tech School (http://authorstechschool.com) Use code ICANLEARN at checkout.

WordPress for Beginners

Are you an author or blogger who struggles with the technical side of your website? Do you wish you could change the layout of your website but are afraid you'll break it?

In "WordPress for Beginners," you'll learn how to build a beautiful, functional website in WordPress. This course is designed just for authors or bloggers who have little to no technical experience, so you don't need any prior knowledge. Your instructor, Barb Drozdowich, uses easy-to-follow directions with specific examples so you'll be able to get started on your website right away.

When you sign up for "WordPress for Beginners," you'll get immediate access to more than 8 hours of content covering topics such as:

- Choosing a hosting company and get your website going
- Understanding the basics of WordPress: logging in, layouts, settings, etc.
- Using themes and plugins
- Protecting your site from hackers and spammers
- Making sure your website looks great on any browser or phone
- Backing up your website

Once you have the basics down, there are even a few advanced topics to build upon what you've learned, like using Google Analytics to track your content performance and setting up search engine optimization (SEO).

If you are an author or blogger looking to build a brand-new website or enhance the one you already have, don't let your lack of confidence stop you. Sign up and get started on that shiny new site today! The shortened link to the course is: https://geni.us/kY7K4L

WordPress Dot Com for Beginners

Whether you're looking to start a blog or put together a website for your small business, figuring out how to actually get going can feel like a tall task.

But it doesn't have to be.

In "WordPress.com for Beginners," you'll learn everything you need to know to get a website up and running on the free version of WordPress. The course includes 25 easy-to-understand videos that guide you through each step, from creating an account to setting up your site to publishing your first post.

When you sign up for "WordPress.com for Beginners," you'll get immediate access to more than 3 hours of content covering topics such as:

- Setting up your WordPress.com account
- The difference between pages and posts and how to publish content on them
- A walk-through of 4 different themes and how to use them on your website
- How to manage comments and give other people access to your website
- What are widgets and how can they improve your site

There are even a few freebies and plenty of other resources along the way to set you up for success.

If you've made the decision to launch your own website, don't let the technology scare you away. Sign up today and start publishing your content in no time! The shortened link to the course is: https://geni.us/P9zt8

Mailerlite for Beginners

If you sell a product or offer a service, you should also have a mailing list. It's the best way to get information out to your audience, share offers, and turn enthusiastic fans into paying customers. People who have signed up for your newsletter are already interested in what you have to say and are much more likely to pay attention to what you have to offer than if they stumble across an ad on social media.

Once you start collecting email addresses, you'll want to sign up for a newsletter service that can send customized emails to multiple people at a time.

In “Mailerlite for Beginners,” you’ll learn all about one of the simpler newsletter services, Mailerlite. Your instructor, Barb Drozdowich, will walk you through the steps from how to navigate the dashboard, how to create a campaign (a newsletter), how to create signup forms, and more.

When you sign up, you’ll have immediate access to 19 videos that cover everything you need to know to get started, such as:

- The legalities you need to know about (opt-ins and opt-outs, what the GDPR is and what it means for you)
- How to set up your account
- Managing your subscribers
- How to create a campaign and send out a newsletter
- How to run reports to see what percentage of people are opening your emails and clicking on the links within your newsletters

You’ll also get plenty of resources for more information and support once the course is over.

Learning something new can feel overwhelming, but it doesn’t have to be. Sign up and start connecting with your potential customers today! The shortened link to the course is: https://geni.us/MLbeginner

---

How to Self-Publish a Book

Each year, more and more authors are realizing that they don’t have to take the traditional publishing route to get their work out into the world. Self-publishing is a great option for many writers, but the actual process of publishing a book yourself can feel overwhelming.

So overwhelming that you might not ever get started in the first place.

In “How to Self-Publish a Book,” you’ll learn everything from putting together your manuscript to getting an ISBN number to formatting and distributing your book. The easy-to-understand, step-by-step format will guide you through the entire process. Before you know it, you'll be sharing your brand new book with your friends and family!

When you sign up for "How to Self-Publish a Book", you'll get immediate access to 19 videos (more than two hours of content!) that cover key topics such as:

• How the publishing industry has changed and what that means for potential authors

• All aspects of publishing: Writing, editing, designing, formatting, uploading, marketing

• What you need to know about file formats

• The necessary pieces to include in a book file

• Where to sell your book

• Red flags to look for if you go with a self-publishing service

Plus, plenty of additional links and resources along the way for even more information.

Don't let what you don't know stop you. Sign up today and finally become the published author you've always dreamed of! The shortened link to the course is: https://geni.us/SelfPublish

---

Website Tips & Tricks - 15 Lessons to Supercharge Your Author Website

You've finally figured out how to create a website to promote your book—great! But once you set it up, how will people find you? What are readers looking for anyway? How do you fix it if something looks off?

The answers are easier than you think.

In "Website Tips & Tricks," you'll gain access to a ton of useful skills to build upon the foundation you already have and maintain your site throughout the years. It's designed for authors who have very little technical knowledge, and you can implement what you learn right away.

Just a few of the topics include:

• The three pages your website absolutely must have

• Choosing your theme and plugins

• Creating content that is reader-friendly and highlights your books

• Setting up your website so it loads faster

• Improving your website's visibility in searches

Most importantly, you'll become comfortable playing around with your website.

Your instructor is Barb Drozdowich, who has published 27 books on a variety of tech topics, including 7 about software and technology. She teaches several online courses and has 50+ YouTube videos, all focusing on making technology easier for beginners to understand. She breaks complex topics down into simple steps so that you can use what you learn right away.

Managing your website doesn't have to be scary. Sign up for immediate access to "Website Tips & Tricks" and start improving your site today! The shortlink to the course is: https://geni.us/WebsiteSupercharge

Printed in Great Britain
by Amazon